GIVEN AWAY

To Matt!

Kate Anne Kang ♡

GIVEN AWAY

Kate Anne Kang

ISBN-13: 9780692790991
ISBN-10: 0692790993

This book is dedicated to Omma,
I'm sorry it took so long. Saraenghashimnika.

To Oppa,
For following through on your promises. Kamsahashimnika.

In Loving Memory of
Janice Helen Carlson Strand

Korea, 1969

DEAR.

I am going to tell you, Please don't forget my talk.

I sincerely hope that you will just take care of Anny and love her like your babies.

In future, please write me a letter often as you can possible to my under address.

So than I will write to you.

P.S. I am Anny's Mother. (Kang, Shin-Hae)

‿ᴄ

September 1991

It began with a telephone call and my adoptive mom's excited words, "Katie...Kate, I have terrific news...your Korean family is looking for you!"

On my end of the line, her words were meaningless, incomprehensible to me. My mom might as well have spoken Swedish, Martian, *Korean* for all I understood.

It was late afternoon, my north facing studio apartment was shrouded in the waning light of day, but everything went black. At some point I realized I was lying on the wooden floor tangled up in my green telephone cord. The words my mom said looped over and over in my insensible mind, loose alphabets began to float and bob on the darkened ceiling. Letters gathered, aligned, formed a sentence, and like a string of Christmas lights, flashed: *Your Korean family is looking for you....*

Those were the very words I had wanted to hear. But twenty-two years later, I stopped thinking about that life. My before life, with my before mother. That was history, ancient history left for ruin. Buried deep, it was all but forgotten.

But as I lay on the floor, a curtain of hazy memories lifted, and images, scenes began to play out in front of me. A thought rocketed and flared: *she hasn't forgotten me after all.* Then. *No, she hasn't forgotten Anny. But Anny doesn't exist anymore.*

༜

Part One
ADRIFT

These fragments
I have shored against my ruin.

T.S. ELIOT

1

Korea Social Service Inc., February 13, 1969
Recommendation:
Anny was referred to our office for support of her care by her natural mother. She is legally free for adoption abroad, and seems to be eligible for adoption in terms of her health and of her personality...it is recommended she be selected for a proper adoptive home.

September 24, 1969

Her mother explains ways to avoid bad luck when she gets *there, there, there,* but the words make no sense to her. Instead of listening to her, Anny takes in the frenzied activity of the city outside the cab window: fast cars, tall buildings lost in clouds, throngs of people clogging the streets of Seoul.

They arrive at a building, but her mother is not ready to enter. She squats down in front of her daughter and fusses with the girl's salon-styled hair. Coaxes dark stray strands into place with her fingers. Straightens her red dress, re-ties her cotton sash. Worries over the cold sore at the corner of her mouth.

She tries to stand still, to let her mother do what she always does, to dote and hover over her. But the deafening roar in the sky is too much. She covers her ears, closes her eyes.

Come, Anny, come. It is time.

Inside, children weep. Cling to adults. Others kick and scream on the dirty floor. An acrid, musky smell fills the tense room. Anny tries to grab hold of her mother's hand. But she is on the wrong side. Her mother's unusable arm is tucked in the pocket of her skirt. She darts behind her mother's legs.

An apparition, with yellowwhitehair and eyeslightblue approaches her mother. They speak in a language she does not understand. The pale woman kneels down and says something to her. She has never seen such yellowhair. Seethroughblueeyes. With an outstretched hand, the woman lures her out from behind her mother. She continues to gape up at her whiteness, her exotic words.

Hot air, outside air. She is outside. Her mother! Where is her mother? She tries to wrench her hand free, but the stranger will not let go.

Omma! Omma! Unable to see her mother, she hears her voice, her mother's last words, *Anny, be a good girl. Go to school. Be good.*

Where is she going? Why does she have to go? Is she a bad girl? Now she has questions, so many questions. But the words will not loosen from her tight throat.

September 24, 1969
Minneapolis-St. Paul Airport.

She is awakened abruptly. *Hurry, hurry, we are here.* The woman's rushed words, quick movements, frighten her all over again. Unload the children. The babies. Go, go go. *The woman. Stay close to the woman. Clutch her hand.* She is led off the airplane, down a dark tunnel into a brightly lit room. Shouting. Crying all around her. Pop pop pop of flashbulbs, daze and blind her. Strangers clamor, grab at shrieking immigrant children. *The woman's arm, hold tight to her arm. Don't let go.*

Before she can react, a ghostly man grabs her. She recoils. Tries to hide behind the woman, but he holds her tight. He picks her up, embraces her. Crazed with fear she thrashes wildly, attempts to leap from his arms. Her fingers claw him. Beat him beat him. Her wails turn to screams, into words, *No. No. Omma. Omma. Odie, Omma?*

The man digs in his pocket with one hand, the other arm tight around her as she continues to flail. A woman comes to his aid. She slips a coin into a machine, thrusts a chocolate bar at her, an appeasement. But she cannot be bribed into calmness, quiet. She flings the candy. The chocolate bar breaks into pieces as it skids across the airport floor.

A missed photo opportunity: She, between two light-haired boys. In front a younger girl with flyawaywhitehair. The woman and man stand behind, each with a hand on her shoulder. Her large Asian eyes, weary, defeated, haunted. A faint trace of salt-dried tears visible down her cheeks, chin, neck. The cold sore, raw, an angry red. Her dress wrinkled, sash undone. From the long journey, from fitful sleep, from wrestling with the man, her hair a tangled mess.

Yet, her first, and lasting impression will not be found in a photograph, but remembered as if viewing an overexposed negative. Against a black background, a translucent, white, indistinguishable mass. Her new family.

Early morning, she wakes, frightened by her strange surroundings. Seeking solace, comfort, she remembers something the man did as he carried her into the house in the night. She wanders, finds the room, drags a wooden stool to the refrigerator, climbs up until her fingers find it. Sitting on the stool, she unwraps the crinkled paper. Picks up a broken piece of chocolate, bites into sweetness. A taste of home. *Omma?* With eyes closed, an image of her mother appears. *When are you coming to get me?* Her mother smiles but does not speak.

She will wait. She will wait for her mother to bring her back to Korea.

﹍ᴓ

Korea Social Service Inc. February 13, 1969
<u>*Description of Child*</u>*:*
Anny is a good natured, cheerful and active little girl. She responds wonderfully to strangers and is able to make friends easily and quickly. At the Reception Home, from the first day of her entry into the Home she was able to get along well with the housemothers and children as if she had been there previously....

In the first weeks of her new life, she curls herself in a fetal position, in a green armchair, in a living room. From there she is able to look out a large picture window. She cannot be moved from this spot. She wants to be able to see her Omma walk up to the front door. She does not understand why her mother has not come for her yet. She cannot understand anything at all: the strange house, the people in the house, the words they speak. She buries her head in the soft cushion, presses her hands over her ears to block out the sounds of their language. She wants to hear only her Omma's voice, her own language.

The new mother brings her a sandwich, sets the gold metal tray on a side table. The sandwich remains untouched. She calls out for *mul*, water, and cries in frustration when the mother brings milk instead. Her concerned blueeyes behind blackcateye glasses linger over the girl, waiting and watching.

The father, in pastor's attire, black shirt with white collar, kneels down in front of her, clearblueeyes behind black-rimmed glasses. He moves his mouth but the incoherent sounds tire her. She turns away, buries herself in the chair cushion. She waits for him to leave.

The older boy, Peter, nine, sits cross-legged on the floor by the chair and chooses simple words in his one way conversation. Tim, six, mimics his brother's actions. The boys eventually tire of their new sister's hunched and unresponsive back. They play checkers, monopoly, cards to occupy the time until she comes around.

AnnMarie, four, wispywhitehair floating in all directions, eventually gets her dark sister's attention. Her largeblueeyes see the world through her older sister's frightened ones. She comes and holds her hand. With her other hand she points to objects in the room and names them. Eventually she leads her outside. Again the younger girl names objects. The sister with no language repeats after her.

Over time she is willing to move from the living room to the leather recliner in the den. Her family hopes watching television will help her to learn English and lessen her crying. The girl is content for a time to watch whatever is on the black and white screen. She takes delight in the silly antics of Curly and Mo, where comedic punches and slaps need no translation.

One day, a steady stream of boys and girls march into the den, interrupting her solitude. They look surprisingly similar to the Little

Rascals she enjoys watching on the television. The children walk slowly around the recliner, look the newcomer up and down, silently file out of the room and out the front door. The last boy, with a face full of freckles and mischief, takes particular care to inspect her. With hand on his chin in deep concentration, as if in imitation of a judge determining the best specimen, an exotic species at the zoo, a barn animal groomed for display at the Minnesota State Fair. He examines her face. Her hair. Her ten toes dangling over the chair. He gives a final nod and joins the others.

⸗

Her family calls her Katie. She does not heed the change of name, trapped, instead, in a muffled undercurrent. In limbo, she tosses and tumbles. Anny. Katie. Katie. Katie. Cloistered in blackened depths, a temporary protection from a brokenness outside her understanding.

⸗

Weeks later, her parents send her to school in muted numbness, with her brothers. The Scandinavian town is small, but large enough to have both a public school and a private catholic school. With a Lutheran pastor father, she and her siblings attend the public institution. Peter to his fourth grade classroom, Tim to one of the first grade rooms, Katie to the other.

Some of the girls in her classroom decide they will be her protectors from the chaos of school life. Their dark friend who came from a place they have never heard of needs them. This is their opportunity to play house with a real live girl they can care for! It is their calling and they will raise her right.

The girls flit about like mother birds making a nest for their young, bounce from group to group, to teacher, to other classrooms to spread the word of their new role and what this entails. A fortress of desks surrounds her, access met with frowns and determined resistance, a constant murmur as her protectors forge plans for her safety.

Special permission is granted to take her to the cafeteria and recess five minutes before the others. Surely the teachers can understand how confusing the lunchroom is to their friend without words. The girls will speak for her. Without language, they determine she is unable to carry her lunch tray; one of her many saviors will take on the task. The teachers understand, but in gym class, Mr. Hanson has had enough of the girls quibbling over who is to be Katie's partner.

_6

Anny/Katie holds her breath for weeks. Waiting. Watching. Learning. Then, one day, like a diver rising slowly she ascends from the depths. At last it is Katie who surfaces out of the murk. I watch the ripples of my own making undulate out, out, out.

_6

My first memory I recall is confirmed in a photograph and on film. It is my seventh birthday. I wear a red and white gingham checked smock worn at mealtime to protect my good clothes, my practical mom explained. Underneath the smock I wear a new white dress with a flouncy pink and pale green skirt tied at my hip by a wide shiny pink sash. I will wear my beautiful dress long after I outgrow it. A wide red plastic headband holds my Jackie Kennedy hairstyle, the ends flipped under rather than up. On my Korean face is a delirious expression. Towering in front of me on the dining room table, on a glass stemmed plate, is an enormous chocolate cake with seven lit white candles. This tradition captivates me since it involves chocolate cake, my favorite treat.

This celebration is also captured Zapruder style, on 8mm colored film, with no sound. My dad is filming this occasion. Peter, Tim, AnnMarie, and mom sit at the dining room table singing *Happy Birthday* to me. I look around at my American family. In two months I have come to accept my new life. The transformation is made complete with my name change from Anny Kang to Katie Strand. In my mid-twenties, I will insist that everyone call me Kate. I am learning how to be Swedish-American, like my family. I am learning English quickly, and when we move out of the small town in three months, I will have forgotten most of my Korean words.

My mom says I can blow out the candles. What does she mean? I look blankly at my family. My siblings take turns showing me. Peter, pantomimes blowing out with his lips, his mouth. Tim, who cannot be outdone, joins in, takes in an exaggerated breath, mimics an exhale. AnnMarie leans into the cake and without letting out her breath, pretends to blow. I understand. I look at my mom with an eager-to-please face. My mouth forms the word, *now?* Mom nods. An ecstatic smile exposes a missing bottom front tooth, tiny dimples on each cheek, and on my left, a barely traceable scar. The cold sore has healed and disappeared.

Bouncing up and down I lean in, but the candles are too high on my colossal cake, I must get up on my knees. Golden flames from the seven candles highlight my features. As proof of my new life, my new identity, I fill my lungs with Minnesota air and release the last of my Korean breath.

2

Korea Social Service Inc., February 13, 1969
Family Status:
Anny was born to Korean mother and Caucasian American father, who can not be reached since her birth...and as a fatherless child...she as well as her 2 year-old half-brother, has been cared for by her mother since her birth....

October 1991

A blustery gray morning and I lounged in bed, my day off from the Greek restaurant where I waitress. No commitments lured me from the warmth of my futon mattress. No boyfriend, no new guy, no random fellow lying next to me. I tried to find the positive in being alone. I did not have to make conversation; I could take my time lazing in the mess of sheets and blankets and heap of pillows; a pot of French roast coffee all to myself. I replenished my cup of coffee, slipped in a tape, Cowboy Junkie's *Caution Horses*, and crawled back into the warmth of my bed.

Normally it was habit for me to pull out the atlas and fine-tune my itinerary for next summer's backpacking trip through Europe and parts of Asia; I'd thought of doing this since high school. I hoped to work on a Kibbutz in Israel, take in the tranquility of Nepal, and somewhere between there and Thailand, I hoped to find myself. Over the summer, I added Korea to the travel plan. Which was out of the blue. I was not sure why I did, rarely had I given thought to that country and its people. Yet something *compelled* me to consider it and to put it on the itinerary. Perhaps I thought, *might as well check out the Hermit Kingdom while I'm in that part of the world anyway.*

Having completely disassociated myself with the Korean culture, because there were no Koreans in my community, it was not a stretch to believe Koreans were non-existent in Minnesota. Only later would I discover there was a healthy Korean population, including Korean adoptees living in and around Minneapolis. I would learn that Minnesota has the highest Korean adoption rate in the United States. But, in 1991, Koreans were still fairly invisible.

On that cold fall day, the gray light barely illuminated my apartment. All desire to venture out was blunted by winter's imminent arrival and its many negative implications: Endless shoveling, plowing, skidding on ice, frozen fingers, toes, and snow, snow, snow that would soon dominate my life, a misery I could not seem to reconcile.

However, travel and winter were not the first things on my mind. Instead, I was still grappling with the news of my Korean family. I thought of little else since the phone call from my adoptive mom less than a month ago. I had gone immediately to Lutheran Social Service to sign the requisite forms allowing consent for my Korean family to contact me.

"Now go home and wait for a reply from your family."

What? I thought my Korean family would walk in the room the minute I signed the forms. Where were they, behind the door? Out in the hallway?

"Someone from your Korean family will be in touch with you." No. They did not know who or how long it would be before I received a reply.

Besides my mother, I could not imagine who made up my family. I understood my father was American who left before I was born, so it stated in my adoption papers. I had a younger half brother but he was adopted before me. Could it be that my father found my mother, and now, together, they wanted me back? I reprimanded myself almost twenty-nine years old and still fantasizing like a child!

A favorite childhood fantasy of mine was where my famous *blond-haired mother* came back for me and together we found my younger brother. Of course it would be made into a movie! The scenes involved running in slow motion into the arms of my ultra glamorous, famous mother probably played by Shirley Jones. So chic even Hollywood bowed down to her. This Oscar-winning drama would not be complete without musical scores arranged by Bread (I adored *The Good-bye Girl*), *Beth* by KISS, and countless other sappy songs I loved, *a must*, I would insist before signing with the world renowned director of the moment. Of course, I would make sure Shaun Cassidy got a role too. In the movie version he would somehow be my older boyfriend. Since I never really had a serious boyfriend in elementary school, I would be fine with fictionalizing it a bit, if it meant meeting dreamy Shaun.

Shortly before the news of my family's search for me, Channel 11 news broadcasted a segment on a Korean boy with leukemia in need of a donor. Initially, I was amazed to see a Korean child featured on TV. An Asian face on television was rare, a story about an Asian person rarer still. It seemed matters were complicated because he was adopted; he couldn't count on his adoptive family to be a likely match. I had not thought about my Korean family in years, but I fell into a dream. I saw myself offering to be tested to see if I was a match—which I was—because I was his long lost big sister!

_6

The apartment buzzer jarred me out of my daydream. I peeked out the large floor-to-ceiling window near my bed where I could get a good view of the courtyard and front door three floors below. It was the mailman. I wondered why he was ringing my apartment. I rarely received mail. When I did, it was mainly bills, collection notices, but since my move earlier in the summer, with no forwarding address, collectors hadn't caught up with my current address yet. I could not afford to order anything, so I wasn't expecting a package, which would be, I thought, the only reason for him to ring me. My laziness won out over curiosity. I didn't want to abandon my bed to answer the buzzer. It could wait. He probably had the wrong apartment anyway. I almost forgot to check the mail until later that day.

There was a yellow notification in my mailbox. I had a package waiting for me at the post office. From Korea.

⸻

My fourth grade teacher, Ms. Gustafson, was my favorite. She wore white go-go boots and mod scarves to hold back abundant brown locks, and suggested I write my precious thoughts—she said I had precious thoughts!—in a journal. I did immediately and continued long into the future.

She assigned me Korea for my country report. Although Korea was the last country I wanted to learn about and report on, I did not think less of her. On Around the World Report Day, I was sure the kids would stare at me and think Korea was not a glamorous country, not like France with their berets and baguettes; Italy, with yummy pasta and paintings of naked fat people (gross, but so much to squeal about); or Denmark, the shimmery water world of mermaids, and the beloved Hans Christian Andersen. They would realize that Korea was a poor and sad country. A country where its people gave away their children.

I had to convince my classmates this was a special place, even if I did not believe it myself. Geography: They have lots of mountains! Climate: They have four seasons like Minnesota! It snows so they can ski, too! Instead, I was a girl who liked visuals, accessories that I could exhibit. The red dress and tennis shoes I wore on the airplane looked just like the clothes my American classmates wore, but, my note card stated, *These came all the way from Korea!* I laid out my turquoise and white *hanbok*, a traditional Korean dress and jacket, along with the impossibly narrow blue rubber shoes and under slip, *To wear on holidays!* This made all the girls in my class want to have one too.

In first grade, I had brought my *hanbok* to school for show and tell. I put on the long white cotton under slip, the full skirt, empire waist jacket with wide sleeves that tied in front. But I grew quickly those first years. In just a few months, my pretty hanbok was already too short in the sleeves, the floor length dress now ankle-length. Mom took a picture of me with my flipped under Jackie Kennedy hairstyle held back with a matching white plastic headband. I walked from room to room and had my own one girl show. I was a star for a day. The children *oohed* and *aahed* as I spun around making my skirt flare out to reveal silver birds and fuchsia and pink flowers. I made up a Korean dance for the finale.

For the report, I also displayed a 1970 white nylon calendar with a painting of pine trees silhouetted against haunting Korean mountains. My Korean mother sent it the first year of my adoption.

Mom suggested we make kimchi, a fermented spicy cabbage side dish a staple food in Korea, for observers to taste. I was excited. Not because I liked it, I did not. My palate was too accustomed to hamburgers, hot dogs, and hot dishes. I tasted it once when my parent's friend brought me a small jar. Before mom got the lid off the jar our nostrils had flared, repelled by the odor. Dad left the kitchen none too slowly, we children held our noses, laughed as we agreed the smell was of rot and human toots. But Miss Gustafson told me she loved kimchi, and if she liked it, then I would make it for her. She proclaimed it was the best kimchi she had ever tasted.

But I still did not want to be associated with the country and its people.

While working on my country report, my parents showed me a newspaper article, a story about my adoption that had been written up for the local paper. *7-Year-Old Korean-American Adopted By Pastor's Family.* Underneath the caption, in a black and white photograph, my family smiles for the camera. Everyone, that is, but me. I look miserable. It must have been taken shortly after my seventh birthday; I have the same short hairstyle with the red plastic headband as my birthday picture. The scar on my left cheek is still visible. And two columns over is a school photograph of me with a gap-toothed grin.

Life in Korea had been fairly rugged for the little girl, due to the fact that people of her country have not as yet adjusted to accept persons of mixed races. Even attending school would have been nearly impossible for her.... The Strands report that the little girl was ravenously hungry when she arrived. She has since gained about five pounds.... She is extremely neat, even going so far as to fold her doll's clothes and store them away in neat piles....

Also in the folder was a document, my adoption file, from *Korea Social Service, Inc.*, written in 1969. It was the adoption agency in Korea that partnered with Lutheran Social Service in Minnesota to bring thousands of Korean adoptees to families all over the state. A handful of tissue thin sheets of typed paper summed up my nearly seven-year existence in Korea. My biological father was a Caucasian

American serviceman of unknown origin. He was transferred back to the states before my birth. I was sure I would never meet him or know his ethnicity. I was half Korean and half Caucasian. I had a younger brother. He was two at the time of my adoption. I had no memories of him, but with the information before me, I conjured up a younger brother, so real I could almost see him, with his arms out, crying, as he was carried away, adopted by an American couple, I believed.

Attached to the document was a black and white photograph of me at...five years old? Six? I hardly recognized myself. The girl in the photo had short unkempt hair. Unsmiling. She did not look as though she liked having her picture taken. I imagined the photographer asked her to smile. *Say cheese. Kimchi.* I looked as if I did not take his cue. On the back of the photo was typed, *Kang, Anny. KSS & LSS of Minn.*, and handwritten in pencil, *97*. Was I the ninety seventh child put up for adoption by the agency?

I wondered about my name and the odd spelling of it, Anny with a *y* instead of *ie*. Why had my Korean mother given me an English sounding name? Was it originally a derivative of a Korean name?

My parents had browsed through a book for eligible adoptees and came upon me. "We saw your picture and we knew you were the one," Mom said, holding the picture. "We took out a loan to adopt you."

How did you know I was the one for your family? What made you choose me? What did you see in my unhappy face? Why did you pick a child the same age as your son? Why didn't you adopt a baby? You had to buy me? You had to pay them in order for me to come live with you?

Did I ask any of these questions? No. No, I did not. I was afraid to ask, to know. I was in full denial of my adoption, and asking questions would reinforce the very thing I wanted to bury: that I had been given away. My parents might confess their true feelings towards me, the adoption. I was afraid it would not be all that positive.

Mom mentioned several times throughout my childhood the expense it cost for them to adopt me. I tried to believe it in the very best light; it was her way of saying she was glad that they had done so. No regrets.

‑‑‑6

My mom signed me up for swimming lessons that first winter. If I was going to be near water, a pool, the lake at our cabin, it was necessary to know how to swim. I discovered a love of water, a love of swimming.

My siblings narrated all the fun we would have up north at the cabin: swimming in the lake, swimming down at the dam, canoeing, rowing and motor boating, inner tubing, fishing, blueberry picking and so much more. I could not wait to experience the fun!

But on one of the first days of summer I broke my arm riding in a go-cart with Tim. We rammed into a rock, the go-cart overturned. Tim walked away without a scratch but I ended up in a cast.

It was important that the cast on my right arm remained dry. No swimming in pools. No swimming in the lake at our cabin. My siblings plumbed the waters, jumped off the raft, and lounged in inner tubes out in the middle of the lake, while I sat miserably on the dock dangling my toes, just grazing the water. I dragged my feet through the pebble-sand shoreline. Slowly inched in deeper, to my calves, thighs, waist. Tuned out mom's warnings of, *that's far enough*. She realized it was futile to give me warning after warning. She got a plastic baggy, put my arm inside it, tied it with string and set me loose. It was a compromise of sorts. I could *swim* by keeping my cast arm high out of the water while paddling fiercely with my left arm, kicking double time with my feet.

Mom wrote to my Korean mother that summer. She sent her pictures of me in the white cast, standing shirtless on the shore of the lake.

My Korean mother wrote back. She wanted an explanation. *What happened to Anny? What was the white thing on her arm?* Mom did not know, and could not know, that in my Korean mother's world there were no casts for a broken arm. She wrote back, apologized for frightening her. My broken arm was temporary. It would get better. I scrawled a short thank-you note for the calendar with the grim mountains and pine trees. It was my last contact with her.

‿

The few remaining memories of Korea were fleeting snippets, quick images, a black and white movie trailer where the scenes flashed past in fragmented seconds to hook you into watching the full-length feature. But there was no more of the movie, not enough of the trailer for me to catch the plot. The cast of characters remained incomplete. Only one character appeared in every screen. She had use of one hand and arm. She tucked her withered hand into the waistband of her skirt or pocket. She made kimchi out in a courtyard. She bent over planting long green stalks in a rice field. I cupped my hands around my mouth and called out to her. She stood up and said something back to me. We walked on railroad tracks waiting for someone. At the airport I lost sight of her, momentarily distracted by an enormous silver bird. I stood open-mouthed staring at the dazzling, shining object, awed. As I was led towards its shiny body, I heard my mother's voice for the last time. *Be good.*

I knew I would never get to see that movie from beginning to end, which was fine by me. I no longer wanted to remember any part of that life. There was no time to contemplate or reflect on the first film anyway, another movie has begun. This second show was much better. It was in color, with a full cast of characters, of parents, brothers, a sister, aunts, uncles, cousins, grandparents. The scenes were pleasant, a short time in a small town, then a move to a middle class neighborhood in a good sized house on a corner lot with a spacious backyard, and plenty of friends in the neighborhood. Summers spent at the family cabin. This story took place in the richest country on earth. I was neither poor nor hungry here. They have loaded me with treats, buttered popcorn, large coke, milk duds, as much as I wanted, whenever I wanted. This was the best movie. I was hooked.

3

Korea Social Service, February 13, 1969

<u>Description of Child:</u>

She is fully aware of the fact of being a mixed parentage....Her mother stated that since last January, she has shown interest in going to the US and been inquisitive about the possibility of her adoption abroad....She did ask for her turn of travelling to US many times to the worker. In many ways she seems to be quite well prepared for the seperation from her mother.

October 1991

I sit in my car, in the post office parking lot, holding in my sweaty hands a medium size yellow envelope with a Korean return address and stamps. *Photographs. Do Not Bend* is neatly marked on the front. Photographs? Who would send me photographs? My mother? I'm confused, disoriented. I watch myself from a distance moving in slow motion.

Heavy limbs. Heavier envelope. Shaky hands that belong to me take a lifetime turning over the envelope. On the backside, I cannot find an edge, a place to grab, to tear open. It is sealed with clear adhesive tape for added security which prolongs my mounting anticipation. I cannot get at it. Car keys, a sawing motion, a small opening. Tearing of the envelope, a deafening sound.

Out tumble photographs and a letter. Pictures of people I have never seen before. A young girl on skis in a white jacket and snow pants, another girl in an orange and purple jacket, stands in front of a statue, a female Buddha. Photograph of a family, Koreans presumably. They stand in front of a stone wall, three girls in front, behind them a man in a black leather jacket, a well-dressed woman, and an older woman. They are Asian and foreign to my Minnesota adapted eyes. I do not know who these people are. I think the post office has made a mistake. I must have received someone else's pictures.

But the letter is addressed to me, the former me, Anny Kang, care of Kate Strand. *But then, who are these people?* I look closer and I see a half obscured face behind the oldest girl. It is the face of an older woman. She looks almost familiar. Her face has changed and aged, she wears glasses, her hair, short, tightly curled. Yet. I want to believe that I recognize her...*is she...can she...is she my mother?*

The letter writer says she is. She is my *Omoni,* mother, *Omma,* mom. Her name is Kang, Shin-Hae. Shin-Hae. She is my mother.

Again I look at the woman and from some distant place in my mind, I can almost see her. There are traces of myself in her countenance: large eyes, high cheekbones and a square face. My Mother. *Omoni. Omma. This is my Mother. She is my mother. Mother. Mother....*
Our mother has never forgotten you.

...Neither have I. I am your older brother. Wait. *What? Older brother? I have an older brother?* My mind flits about trying to recall, to conjure up an older brother. I peer closely at his face. I look at the other faces, the woman standing next to him. I don't know who she is. His wife? Again, I look at the man. *My older brother?* I do not remember an older brother. There was no mention of an older brother in my adoption papers. *What older brother?*

I feel as if my head will explode. I cannot focus. My eyes dart among the photographs and the letter. *Mother. Omoni. Omma. Older brother. Older brother. He is my older brother.* I no longer see the photographs. I cannot take in any more words. Letters on the page run into one another and tumble off the paper.

It is coming at me too fast. It's too much. Too much.

My head, dull, sluggish, rests on the steering wheel. Outside the parking lot, dried brown leaves caught in a vortex of late afternoon breeze swirl around my red car. Dead leaves twirl up, dip, rise, dip...a final nose-dive onto the hood, to the black asphalt.

I am nothing like the lightness of leaves; instead, once again, I'm submerged in blackened waters. Heaviness, weariness holds me under. This moment is immense, and I'm not sure I have the strength to do anything beyond sitting in my car. Holding my breath.

I have an older brother.

His name is Jae Il. We have different fathers. His wife is my *eonni,* Korean for sister-in-law. He has three daughters: Fifteen year old Ah Young, Ah Rim, thirteen, and Ah Hee is eleven. They know me as *Komo,* aunt. He claims they are my family.

That single word does me in. *Family.* Is it possible to implode from over-crying? I cannot stop crying. I will surely fill my car with tears. Hammering in my head. Nausea. Runny nose. I need a tissue. But of course I don't have a tissue. A sleeve sops up never ending tears, drippy nose.

I stare at the pictures, will myself to recall moments that include a big brother. I cannot find any scenes. He looks older. Maybe I didn't know him well? I continue to cry at the uncertainty of the situation. *I have an older brother? How could I have forgotten him? Why can't I remember him? Can this be right?* I cannot summon him from my darkened mind.

Every ounce of energy is used up on tears and confusion. Grasping for erased memories has depleted my reserves. To drive out of the post office parking lot feels like a monumental effort. I close my eyes, put my head back on the headrest. I want to go back to my before life. My life before the phone call. My life before the letter. Where I can continue living a half life.

⁓

Korea Social Service Inc., February 13, 1969
Description of Child:
While she was at the Reception Home, she was not choosy with food and had a good appetite; liked to have new clothing and preferred green colour to others and tended to keep her clothings or posessions very clean and neat; and could manage her daily living affairs by her-self without other's help.

Shortly after our move to Saint Louis Park, a classmate gave me a goldfish. I named him Sebastian. He needed a dignified, regal name; it would cheer him up, make him feel important while he swam around and around in his semi-round glass bowl. His glass home was on top of a white bookshelf, under two large windows framed by white eyelet curtains. Every day as I got off the school bus, I looked up at my window and could see Sebastian's bowl. I imagined he saw me waving at him as I ran toward the house.

I burst into the bedroom I shared with AnnMarie, ran over to the bowl and gave him an enthusiastic greeting. Sebastian looked forward to my return from school. I laid on top of my nubby white cotton bedspread and told my friend all about my day. I knew he heard me as he swam around in his green and blue pebbled world.

He came to know all my secrets. I trusted him. Once in a while he stopped swimming and for an instant he looked straight into my eyes. He understood me. We were similar. He knew I lived in a glass bowl too. I was Korean. Except no one knew what a Korean person was or where Korea was in the world. People could easily find China on the globe, so they assumed me Chinese. I was unable to argue the difference. What did I know about Korea?

I knew Sebastian was tired of visitors peering at him with their various shades of blue eyes. They wanted to hold him. Touch him. Caress his scales, his beautiful plume of a tail. They held him too tight, too long. Water. He needed to be back in the water, where he ought to be, swimming in lazy circles, rather than darting crazily like he did after the attention, the fawning. *Where's your momma? She misses you. You're all alone little Sebastian.* The endless chatter of little girls was too much. He shot to the other side of the bowl, as if to escape, his gossamer tail the only sign he was still there.

⟶

That first year I managed my world by managing my possessions, perhaps as a way to feel in control. I started with my clothes. They were hung in the closet according to color: all the blues together, yellows, reds. My dresser drawers were carefully lined with white shelf paper (how I longed for the pink rose or yellow daisy pattern with scented liner, but alas, too impractical, which meant too expensive). The drawers held my perfectly folded white underwear and matching white socks tucked in pairs so as not to stray and mingle with other socks. Sweaters, t-shirts and shirts, folded and stacked in layers, made it possible for each item to be seen upon opening the drawers.

On the bookshelf that dad built and mom painted white, my books were alphabetized from A-Z. A beloved clay statue of Pippi

Longstocking that mom got at a garage sale gave the shelf a sense of fun with her red braids sticking out on either side of her cheerful, expectant freckled face. I felt a kinship with Pippi. She was motherless too. She had a father, but he wasn't around much; she had to grow up by herself. I felt better knowing that at least I had a family to help me grow up. There was something both fascinating and horrifying to be orphaned and completely on one's own. Pippi seemed to handle it; she made the best of her situation. She lived in a world with a different mind-set and I wanted some of that to rub off on me. She could make mistakes seem incidental, entertaining, rather than unforgiveable. If I made them: I could be given away again.

Sebastian, always my faithful friend, poised on the top shelf, guarded my goods from AnnMarie who was known to take my stuff without asking.

To keep a bedroom neat and tidy would win me points in this home. Laying out perfectly folded or hung clothes for the next school day was my salve, my therapy. I didn't think Pippi would have done that. My backpack sat at the ready by the bedroom door lest I forget it. It was packed with finished homework, sharpened pencils, notebooks and folders on which I had spent hours drawing flowers and fairies. Every morning I made my bed as if in training for the army. With great care I smoothed out any unseemly wrinkles and fully covered my pillow with the white cotton bedspread, just like mom showed me. I did my chores without any reminders to clean my room, vacuum the stairs, and dust the living room furniture. I did what I was told. Otherwise, what might be the consequence? I never wanted to find out.

~6~

I hoarded everything. Though it was against the rules, I hid food in the bedroom. But hiding food had to be done stealthily. Who knew how long I would remain in this family? I had been given away once, it could happen again. I needed to be ready for a quick dismissal. My stash was also to satisfy my immediate needs; I was always hungry.

Hiding food was done when I was certain my little sister was not sneaking into my business, which then meant it became mom's business. I made sure my secrets remained undetected: nothing perishable that could rot and be sniffed out. Crackers, anything packaged could be stuffed into socks, back corners of my dresser drawers, behind my dresser, on my three allotted closet shelves, in the pockets of pants and jumpers.

It was when I overheard my parents talking about money, the lack of it, that I became worried. Surely this meant we might go hungry. How long would the food I hid last?

I believed one of the reasons I'd been given away was my mother was too poor to keep me. There probably wasn't enough food and she gave me away so she would have enough. At more benevolent moments, I liked to think she did so for my sake. Later when I read my adoption papers it stated my mother received *the second payment of monthly cash grant under the LSS-KSS Sponsorship Program.... Mrs. Kang has been able to meet her family living expenses for support of Anny offered by our office.* Indeed, we must have been living without.

Was I going to be sent away again? Had I been good? Would they remember the fight Tim and I had? How he yelled at me to go back where I came from, and I had slugged him? Or how angry I got at AnnMarie for getting gum in my long hair, which then needed to be cut much shorter than I wanted? Did they remember the fit I threw when they did nothing to punish her, especially when she acted as though she had done nothing?

My parents started a savings account for me on my seventh birthday. I had $24.75 in that account. It said so in the blue savings book I looked at several times a day. I told myself I would never take money out. It was only for putting money in. But this was an emergency. *My parents needed to pay their bills. They had to buy food.*

Mom and dad were still asleep on an early morning when I knocked on their door. I stood beside my dad's side of the bed. They looked at me in a sleepy haze, tried to focus on which child had woken them at such an ungodly hour. I solemnly held out my savings book.

"What's this? What are you doing?" Dad asked, reaching for his glasses.

"My many dollars in my savings will help with the bills." *We had to have food for dinner.* "You can take out the money right now and get the food. It will pay the bills, too. It's going to be okay because I have a lot of the money."

"It'll be fine, Katie. We will have enough food and the bills will get paid," he said taking off his glasses, lying back on the bed.

I gave him the savings book anyway, though they never touched it. It was my way of contributing. If I helped out maybe they would keep me.

⤳

"Yes, but what *color* green do you see?" I asked AnnMarie from the back seat of our used red Volkswagen Beetle. To talk with her I had to turn and look behind to the cargo space where she got to sit. I coveted that space where only the smallest could fit.

"What do you mean, what color green?" she asked, looking at me like *everybody knows green is green.*

Well, I knew differently. After Ms. Mitchell, my third grade teacher and the best artist in all of Minnesota had informed us of the various shades of green (and blues and yellows and purples). I was dazzled by the possibilities. Did I want my landscape to be colored in hunter green, kelly green, olive green, forest green? I loved having so many choices.

But I was asking Ann Marie and my brothers, who were sandwiched on either side of me—*squishing the daylights out of me*, I had wailed—whether they saw colors the same way I saw them. I was bewildered with kids asking if I saw things the same way they did.

"What do you mean?" I had asked Dan in class.

"You know, with your eyes being funny looking," Dan said. Dean, his identical twin brother, and one of the six boyfriends I had that year, punched him in the arm.

"They're not funny looking." Dean is my favorite at the moment.

"I don't mean funny, I mean 'cuz you got Chinese eyes, they're slanty and smaller than our eyes."

I could not believe what I heard. I didn't know everybody in the world saw my eyes as different. I had fooled myself into believing I was similar to all the blondheaded blueeyed kids, even when people I didn't know stared and continued to look long after passing me.

"Well..." I said to my sister, "like the green on that traffic light. Is it more of a kelly green or a forest green like..." I looked inside the car, nothing but black seats. "Like that billboard, the one for Midwest Bank. What color is that green? Does that green match the green stoplight?"

My brothers thought it was pretty close. So did I!

"Okay, what about that blue car? They call that Robin's egg blue. Is that what it looks like to you?" We knew what robin's egg blue looked like since we found some broken eggshells in our yard that spring. They agreed it was the same color. "I see that same color too!"

"That's stupid. Why wouldn't you?" Peter asked. I explained to them what Dan said.

"Well, do you?" Tim asked, holding my face still so he could look at my eyes. He brought his face within inches of my face, pulled back, turned my head to the left, right, and studied my eyes. He shrugged. He couldn't find anything remarkable about them.

"No, I said, it looks like we see the same colors. But just to make sure, what color purple would you compare my pants to? Is it more like my doll Velvet's headband or...."

―⁓―

Over the years it became routine: the looks, the double takes. At first, it's a glance. Then a long stare to make sure they saw what the mind cannot quite register: an Asian child. Girl. Teenager.

I learned to either have fun or grew irritated with the question, *Where are you from?* The person was really wondering about my ethnicity: was I Chinese? Sometimes they guessed Japanese, then Vietnamese. *I'm from St. Louis Park Minnesota.* It was satisfying to see him or her struggle with this answer. This was not what they expected to hear, and depending on my mood, whether I felt their curiosity was genuine, I would explain where I was born and how I came to be here. Other times I was annoyed with their Minnesota indirectness: ask what you really mean, or I can be vague too.

What's your nationality? I did not know how to answer this question. My *nationality?* Like, where do my allegiances lie? Like, if I had to take up arms, go into battle, would I defend this country? Or was it another version of where are you from?

Go back to where you came from was not an unfamiliar phrase to me. No amount of, *Yes, indeed, I will. I'll be heading back to Saint Louis Park... Minnetonka... Minnesota,* could not take the sting out of those words.

―⁓―

I understood that in order to fit in, I had to remove myself from Anny's story. Anny became a fictitious character in my mind; she was a little girl whose adoption tale I told. She was as much of a character to me as one of the children's stories I grew up on, *Goldilocks, Cinderella, Pippi Longstocking,* or *Heidi,* a Shirley Temple movie about an orphan girl. By the time I was twelve, I was simply Katie, who spoke English and had American friends. Ate American food. Swallowed whole the belief that I, too, was Swedish-American.

Family lore has it when my Sunday school teacher asked the class how many of us were Swedish, I was the first to raise my hand. I saw myself as the good and pious Swedish girl, look past the large brown Asian eyes, straight dark hair, and it would be impossible to find any trace of my former Korean self.

4

Korea Social Service Inc., February 13, 1969
Description of Child:
Anny looks a healthy and good looking girl, who gives the impression of being alert and sensitive. In her physical appearance, she can be easily identified as a child of Caucasian-Korean mixed parentage, and has fair complexion with dark-brown hair and Caucasian-shaped dark-brown eyes. When she smiles, she has dimples on her both cheeks. She is now 45 inches tall with weight of 39.5 pounds.

October 1991

I need to know whether Jae Il is my older brother. My adoption papers said I had a younger brother. How can there be this big of a discrepancy? I have to find out for certain. The next day I send Jae Il a fax letting him know I received his letter and contact information. I will call him tonight at eight o'clock, which in Korea will be fourteen hours ahead making it ten o'clock in the morning the next day. Strange to think that in Korea they will already be experiencing our tomorrow!

I spend an hour pacing in my apartment waiting for the clock to strike eight. I dial his work number. He owns a printing company in Seoul. A woman answers the telephone and says something in Korean.

"Um, Hello. I am calling from America, Minnesota. May I speak to Jae Il?" There is a sharp intake of breath, a long pause.

The woman finally speaks, "Uh...cho...just...a...a...wait...wait, pleaze." Click. I am on hold.

It dawns on me. The woman can barely speak English. I cannot speak Korean. Can Jae Il speak English? How stupid of me to assume they speak English. I am an idiot. My hands are clammy. I'm sweating. How are we going to speak to each other?

The telephone clicks. I hear excited voices in the background. They are speaking Korean. I thought I heard a voice, a deep voice on the line, but I cannot be sure. Silence. There is breathing on the other end, but no one speaks.

"Hello? I am Kate, uh, Anny, calling from Minnesota."

It's the same deep voice. I think he said he is Jae Il, but again I can't be sure. I'm flustered hearing this voice, presumably my brother's, and his Korean words. My nerve has left me. I've forgotten how to speak English. My mouth opens, flaps up and down but no words come out. He doesn't say anything either. He is crying. I start to cry. I grab the long phone cord as if it's my lifeline. I pace in a circle, twisting the cord around my hand.

I'm not sure if it is surprise at hearing Korean words (what was I expecting?) or nervousness at hearing Korean words and not understanding them from someone who claims to be my brother—

I hang up.

I cannot believe I hung up on him! I am a complete moron. Drenched in tears and sweat, my mind roils with confusion at the memory loss of this person I tried to contact. I had hoped hearing his voice might trigger a memory. Nothing.

Overwhelmed, I lie on the dusty floor, crying. *Is he my brother? How can he be my brother?* Why can't I remember him? I have to call him back, but I feel paralyzed with ineptitude. I don't speak Korean and he doesn't speak English. How are we going to communicate? I cannot make the call again and have the same outcome. I cannot do it. I continue lying on the floor, frustrated with myself, when the telephone rings. It is Jae Il. He has an interpreter on the line.

"This is your older brother Jang, Jae Il from Korea," the interpreter said.

"Hello, I am Kate...Anny," I say, in a shaky voice.

Jae Il speaks rapidly to the interpreter. "It has been a long, long time. I have missed you, little sister…Anny," the interpreter relays to me.

My throat constricts, I'm unable to form words. He and I are crying again. At some point I try to say something, to let him know I'm still here. But I still cannot remember how to speak English. Instead I squeak several times to let him know I'm still on the line. I can't stop crying.

After it seems humanly impossible to shed any more tears, Jae Il speaks. He is thirty-eight years old. He did not know I was going to be adopted. At sixteen years old he had to quit school; there was no money for him to continue his education. He and Omma were impoverished and heart-broken; he only had Omma for family until he married at nineteen.

I don't know what to say to this man who believes he's my brother. He seems to know enough of my history to be my kin, but I cannot give up the belief that I had a younger brother.

Without preamble, I ask, "What happened to my younger brother? Do you know where he is?"

Jae Il is confused, baffled by my words. I rephrase the question thinking he doesn't understand, the interpreter doesn't understand what I am asking.

"No. No, little brother," he says several times in English, after I explain that the information from Korea Social Service stated I had a younger brother. Again he says there was no younger brother. Only Jae Il and me.

"Are you sure?" I ask, certain he is mistaken. He again states there is no other brother. There never was a younger brother. He is sorry I believed this all these years.

I cannot take in this information. How could the adoption papers be so wrong? How can this be? But I cannot think about it anymore. My mind shuts down for now. I will think about this later. Not right now.

I called him Jae Il several times during our conversation. The interpreter tells me he is my *Oppa*, which means older brother, big brother, and I should call him this. Koreans do not call each other by name, but rather by birth order. He refers to me as *dongsaeng*, little sister.

I tell him my name was Katie growing up, but now my friends and family try to remember to call me Kate. He wants to know why my name is no longer Anny. I explain my younger sister's name is AnnMarie, and with such similar names, mine was changed. Anne is my middle name. I hear his exclamation of surprise, and the drop in his voice. He says he is sorry that my name was changed. His concern and disappointment over my name change quells any doubts I have. He is my brother.

I enjoy Oppa's voice, especially when he speaks Korean: he sounds authoritative and certain. I try to recognize his voice, his face from my childhood. I cannot. I remember nothing.

―❦

"What's wrong with me? How could I have forgotten my older brother? Forgotten Oppa? Am I heartless? I have no soul," I lament to my long-suffering girlfriends who assure me over many bottles of wine and over beer and margaritas that I'm not heartless and that I do, too, have a soul. Forgetting him was what a six-year-old girl had to do to survive in her new American family.

―❦

From the first phone call in October to nearly Christmas, Oppa and I take turns calling each other. He tells me he is learning English. He listens to tapes on his drive to work. I am trying to learn Korean, and he is pleased. Peter and his wife, Judy, along with her parents, and an uncle, are paying for my Korean lessons. Reconnecting with Oppa has not only brought joy to me, but to my immediate family and extended family as well. It brings out the best in all of us.

Oppa says he wants me to come to Korea. I tell him about my travels, that I had hoped to make Korea my last stop on a year long trip I'd been planning. I was leaving next summer.

If I was honest with myself, I would have acknowledged that my travels were to escape. Whenever I butted up against uncertainty, felt afraid to move forward, I'd browse through the atlas, and turn the pages to Europe and Asia. I would work on a Kibbutz in Israel and see if communal living was the answer. Find serenity in Nepal. Something meaningful I could involve myself with in Thailand. Any place, anywhere to feel a sense of purpose.

Korea was to be the last stop. To seek out my mother was not part of the plan, was never a realistic consideration. The chance of locating her was akin to finding a needle in a haystack.

"You are coming to Korea?" Oppa says. He is excited. "I start looking for you this past summer."

"*This* past summer?" I ask, surprised. He tells me he began his search in early summer, once he felt he had his affairs in order. "Oppa, I decided to add Korea to my travel plans early this past summer too."

We are incredulous at the coincidence of our timing. *We did this at nearly the same time.*

He is silent. I hear pages turning. He is riffling through a Korean English dictionary looking for the right words. He says something in English, but I can't understand him. He says it again.

Telepathy. He is rapidly turning pages again. *Blood is thicker than water.* He believes it is because of our familial connection, a bond between us as brother and sister that explains our simultaneous timing in the search for the other.

I cannot find any rationale, logic to explain this coincidence in timing. How could it be telepathy between us? I had forgotten him. He did not exist to me.

However, I am eager to find an explanation to the compulsion I felt in adding Korea to my travel plans. It was a *sensation*, a *something* hovering over me, a *sense* that *something* was about to happen. It began in late spring and stayed with me all summer. I had no idea what it was. I chalked it up to a deepening depression.

I laugh, hoping it doesn't sound ironic. "That's a beautiful thought. Yes, telepathy. Blood, thicker than water."...

We decide together, I am to go to Korea in the spring.

⸻

Oppa and I have established a pattern of communication so we no longer use an interpreter. At times we labor to understand each other but it is worth it to speak directly to him. Oppa tells me the next time he calls Omma will be at his house. She does not live with him and his wife. She likes living alone in another city, Ansan.

"She must be my mother, I like my own space too." It is the first time I hear him laugh. It makes me smile.

He only recently told Omma that he had found me. She did not know he was searching for me. He did not want to raise her hopes in case he was unsuccessful in his efforts. Eager to speak to me, she has been unable to sleep since hearing the news.

"We must be related, I can't sleep either." Oppa's deep organic laugh gives me goose bumps. I make a mental note to make him laugh more often.

"Anny…" he says, his voice dropping, "Omma…hard life. It bad, bad, you go America. She don't eat, sleep, nothing. She cry. She cry… long time." Oppa chokes up, unable to say anymore.

Tears will be the language that binds us.

5

When I was twelve I was sick for a week, during winter break, no less. I was confined to my bed where I did nothing but sleep. Thoughts of PeggyDebbieDeanne having all the fun without me upset me greatly. After several days, mom said I could come out of my room. The quarantine was lifted. I shivered on the couch under several layers of blankets, where I tried to read, but it was difficult to hold a book and stay warm at the same time.

Mom came in to check on me. Of course AnnMarie wasn't far behind her. AnnMarie stuck close to mom. Mom felt my head, "Do you want some more chicken noodle soup?" I shook my head.

"No. I'm okay."

Mom sat down in a chair and AnnMarie climbed onto her lap. I pretended I was reading, but I was watching them. Mom had her arms around my sister, AnnMarie's head on mom's shoulder. I did not hear what they were talking about, because they spoke quietly, like I was not supposed to hear their private conversation.

Mom let out a light laugh and then she leaned over to kiss AnnMarie's cheek. My cheeks flushed. My heart pounded. I pretended to read my less than riveting book. Mom gave my sister another squeeze and another peck on the cheek. I had never seen mom give out kisses. I was hopeful I'd get one too. My heart was popping like firecrackers on the Fourth of July. I wanted mom's affection, too. "Okay, honey. Let's make sure we have enough Christmas cookies." My sister jumped down from her lap and headed for the kitchen with Mom trailing close behind.

I wished mom would call me honey. I yearned to be called honey. It seemed like a word to say to someone you loved.

The doorbell rang. AnnMarie ran to open the door. "Merry Christmas! Merry Christmas!" Their voices sounded familiar. They were Christmas carolers. *Jingle Bells, Jingle Bells....*

Mom went to the door. "Katie, it's your friends." She started to tell them I was too sick to come to the door.

"No, I'm not," I said heading for the door, wrapped in a blanket.

"Only for a minute, Katie."

PeggyDebbieDeanne and three other friends stood outside the door with big smiles on their friendly faces. "Merry Christmas, Katie! How're you feeling? We miss you! We thought we'd cheer you up with some Christmas songs!"

I smiled at seeing my friends, their enthusiasm. They hadn't forgotten about me after all. After a loud rendition of *Santa Claus Is Coming To Town*, mom told them I had to go back to bed. "Merry Christmas! Merry Christmas! I'll call all of you the minute I'm better. See you soon!"

I had nice friends. But I think I would have traded them all for one *honey* from mom.

⸻

It seemed I was grounded on a regular basis by the time I was ten. When grounded, the rule was you served your time up in your room. You did not commingle with the other family members who can behave, who did not raise their voices, did not talk back. You were allowed to come down at mealtime, to do your chores, but after you were done, you resumed the rest of your confinement in your room.

I usually did not mind my groundings. It gave me time to catch my breath. Between my sports activities, softball, basketball, soccer and swim team, flute lessons, directing a play (The Wizard of Oz), talking on the telephone, and going over to PeggyDebbieDeanne's house, I was scheduled out. This was me time.

My activities during the exile were many. I drew. I adored drawing flowers and fairies and butterflies on my school folders. I had a stack of them to do, AnnMarie and my friends wanted me to draw and color on their folders too. It was also an opportune time to read the numerous books I took out from the library. I could write in my journal. I might perfect making different faces in the mirror. In my young mind I hoped my repertoire of practiced expressions would somehow deflect attention from my Asian features.

I stood sideways in front of the tall mirror that hung over AnnMarie's dresser, pivoted a bit and then expressed. To convey the look of surprise I widened my eyes, situated my mouth into a loose O and lightly placed a hand on a part of my face. Concern: cock the head in the slightest gesture, make your eyes look sad with a bit of consternation mixed in just so. Joy was self-explanatory: you bubble over with enthusiasm. Humility was tough to express, one I did not fully understand. It seemed to involve standing very still, no gesturing, which might lead to exuberant behavior. Drop the shoulders, and lower the gaze, which then made it difficult to see what expression was achieved.

I spent hours perfecting these looks and mannerisms, to view myself as others did when they looked at me. It was rare to see an Asian face, so when someone did, it provoked long stares and comments. I also thought it would pay off when I became an actress or a model. My time was well spent while waiting to be furloughed, where once again I could be among the good people.

Upon my umpteenth confinement, for what, I did not remember. Most likely I did not agree with what my mom told me to do, we argued, I talked back, my dad got involved, told me to go to my room. I refused. I fought him all the way up the stairs by spreading my hands and feet against the walls to block him, to hinder him from bodily moving me. He spanked, dragged and pulled me up to my room. It was more out of principle than dislike at being confined to my room that I made a scene.

I lounged on top of my perfectly made bed, reading *Are You There God, It's Me, Margaret?* Margaret and me, we could have been best friends. I was daydreaming about my non-existent breasts and how doing the you-must, you-must, you-must-increase-your-bust exercise Margaret swore worked, might just work for me too. It was mid-morning and I had the whole day to read and draw and try on sweaters and strut around my room pretending to be a fashion model.

Without warning, the door flew open with such force it smacked against the wall, tearing the wallpaper. A blur came towards me. It was Mom. She pounced on my bed, and towered over me. She thrust her index finger an inch from my face, tried to say something, but for what seemed a long time, she was too upset to speak.

"You think you're a princess," she finally said between clenched teeth. "You think you're some kind of a queen, don't you, sitting up here on your bed, reading your book, not giving a damn about how I'm feeling. How dare you sit here like you're something special," she said. Her knotted face was close, too close to mine. I could feel her saliva as she spit out her words. She breathed heavily on me. She looked at me but she didn't seem to see me.

I was stunned and stung by her words, surprised by her anger. Without thinking, I kicked her hard in the stomach. She fell off the bed, but landed on her feet. I think we were both shocked by my physical aggression. Out of reflex, she grabbed the first thing her hand could reach, my leg. I kicked and flailed and tried to loosen her hold on me. She tightened her grip. I kicked her with my other foot. She said something. I did not hear her. I yelled at her. She continued to hold my leg.

"Let go of my leg, you bitch."

Mom let go.

We looked at each other in silence. Her face had lost its anger. She was shocked at my outburst, my swearing.

"I...I...," but I couldn't seem to get words out. The look on her face scared me.

Mom continued to eyeball me, her face deadened. I shut my mouth and stared back at her.

"I think it's important to forgive, Katie. But it will be harder to forget. I will not be able to forget what you said or did."

I watched her walk out and quietly closed the door behind her.

To this day I cannot recall what I did to provoke that strong of a reaction from her. I am sure I talked back to her, yelled and screamed at her, which had become my defense, my way to handle conflict. I had learned to fight, both physically and verbally, if I felt mistreated. I was not one to start a fight, but often I ended it with the last punch or harsh word.

⸺⸻

I held no memories, no scenes of mom and I enjoying each other's company or sharing mutual delights. Instead, ours continued to be a relationship fraught with arguments and commands to toe the line of family rules.

Mom's good friend, Heidi, was almost a second mom to me. She had three children of her own, her son the same age as Tim and me. Yet she made time for me. One time, I came home with a girlfriend from college to celebrate my birthday. But mom had undergone surgery and was not feeling strong. Heidi offered to make my birthday dinner with all my favorites: lasagna, garlic bread, and salad. For my birthday cake she made a massive black forest cake dotted with liqueur filled cherries she brought back from Germany. She made me feel special.

At Heidi's invitation, we went out for lunch every so often. One such time, in high school, after she dropped me off at home, I found Mom in the garden picking weeds. She wanted to know how my time was with Heidi.

"Fine. I like talking with her. I told her we didn't get along very well and I didn't know what to do about that."

"You what?" Mom straightened up, her face contorted in anger. "You do not tell my friend about our relationship. That's private. That's between you and me. Do you understand me?" She raised her voice, an all too common occurrence whenever she and I talked.

"But she asked how I was and I wanted her advice. She seems to have a good relationship with her kids, I wanted to know what I could do about ours."

"She must think I'm a terrible mother. Did you tell her I was?" She was angrier than I had seen before.

"No, of course not. She thinks it's pretty normal. She's having trouble with Susan, and she expects it'll pass," I said.

Her stony expression told me we were done talking. Mom's garden, a bounty of pink and red zinnias, orange nasturtiums, pink, and yellow snapdragons seemed to drain of color.

I would like to believe it was a sign of the times; mothers mothered and daughters stayed out of their way, telling themselves they'd be nothing like their mother. Is that not the natural cycle? Mom was doing her job: taking care of four children, and by my junior year in high school, she worked part-time outside the home. Mom's high standards of maintaining a beautiful home, cooking meals from scratch, and looking after AnnMarie's needs took up all her time and energy. It did not occur to me until much later in life that my mom and I could work towards having a peaceful relationship.

⎯⊷⎯

If I thought about my Korean mother, it was when I was in conflict with my parents and the level of injustice they meted out. If I was grounded for longer than was warranted for an alleged offense, when I was not allowed an opportunity to defend my side of the story, usually involving a tangle with AnnMarie, I fantasized about all the ways my mother glamorously came to my rescue. Of course she resembled the latest movie or TV star. Our first colored TV in 1971 set in motion a kaleidoscope of fantasies and unattainable dreams.

My fantasy mother had an uncanny resemblance to Glinda, the good witch, with her own enormous pink gown, sparkly crown and magical wand. Or she was pert Laurie from *Oklahoma!* with blond curls swept up in a sassy ponytail; or cool and calm Shirley Jones from *The Partridge Family*. And for a time I thought it would be groovy to have easy-going Florence Henderson with her brood of six kids for a mom.

My daydreams of a biological mother with blondhair and blueeyes were never in doubt. After all, practically everyone around me had those features: my mom, aunts, cousins, moms in the neighborhood.

Knowing I was half Caucasian meant that I, too, could still hope to attain those coveted features. Didn't Caucasian mean whiteskin, blueeyes and blondhair? My hair could still miraculously turn blond, my eyes a beautiful skyblue, probably about the same time my biological mother would sweep me away to her huge mansion near the Pacific Ocean. I was not sure how the physical transformation would occur. Even with a narrow understanding of genetics, I must have known this was not possible, but I wasn't much for details—or reality. Sometimes the act of losing myself in dreams was satisfying enough.

This fantasy of turning blond and blueeyed deepened when I read a story of how this might happen. Whether I read this in the National Enquirer or a legitimate newspaper, I cannot say. Did I know the difference? It was a story of a white couple who gave birth to a dark skinned baby with curly black hair. The baby was a surprise being that the couple was Caucasian. They could prove no moral failings on the wife's part as to the reason for this black child. A sound explanation was determined: Long ago one of the ancestors was a slave and had a child by the slave owner, who then passed for white, as did her children. This continued for several generations to the point that the family buried their black heritage.

The article said the black child had come about due to a latent this, dormant that or recessive/dominant genes, something scientific, *blah, blah, blah*. I didn't really need to know the details, I was sold on the idea, and I knew this was going to happen to me too.

Being half Korean and half Caucasian, turning blond and even blueeyed did not seem that much of a stretch. It would be like outgrowing baby fat (and that, too, could hurry up and happen) with nothing but maybe a hint of my former chubby self left as a reminder. My Korean features would recede and diminish, and at last, I would have Caucasian features.

The day my mother came for me would be the day I'd transform into a Caucasian darling. I would have my coveted blueeyes and blondhair and life would proceed according to my whims. I kept the article for some time, thinking that when people witnessed my transformation I would ever so casually toss them the article in lieu of an explanation, along with a bored expression on my ivory face that said, *read it and weep.*

It was shortly after reading this article and believing with all my heart that a lighter and brighter me was days away, I blurted out to my class that Marilyn Monroe was my mother. My classmates had a good laugh, and then one of the mean ones accused me of being a *chink* so there was no way Marilyn could be my mother. I had no idea what a chink was, but the way he said it I knew I did not want to be one. The ugly word formed a lasting impression that being Asian was bad; I must, at all cost make myself become something else.

Turning into a cute blondheaded girl could not happen fast enough. I permed and teased and lightened my dark brown hair that others erroneously referred to as black. By the time I left for college, and stopped short of actually coloring my hair blond, I eagerly embraced all looks Farah Fawcett. Except there was no way I could make my "feathered" hair behave anything remotely like Farah's. Instead, my heavy hair fell stubbornly over my face. No amount of Dippety Do or Clairol hairspray could tame my slippery follicles to align with my new persona.

⸺⸙⸺

On a rare occasion, I dared to peer into my darkest thoughts, my deepest fears. Why had I been given away? Children asked me or my mom why my Korean mother gave me away—*I mean have you adopted,* they'd say, often times embarrassed at the slip up.

Given away. To my ears it sounded as if I had been thrown away. Gotten rid of. Disposed of. She did not want me. The thought stuck: I was given away. I believed I was given away long before I accepted the word adopted. But why? Why was I given away at almost seven?

I remembered my Korean mother's last words to me, *be a good girl.* I must have been a bad girl. Maybe I was given away because I was an awful child.

6

Korea Social Service Inc., February 13, 1969

<u>*Description of Child:*</u>

Her emotional attachment to her mother appears to be rather less than an average child of the same age. Anny is able to express her needs or demands to her housemother freely, and in such a case as her demand is not to be met, she tends to become sullen for quite a long time. But she usually responds wonderfully and likes to follow suggestions....

December 1991

A few days before Christmas, Oppa telephones me but there is no opportunity to speak to him. I hear another voice, a woman's voice, in the background. His words fade away as someone shouts in to the telephone.

"Anny! Anny!"

"Yes?"

"Anny! Oh my god, Anny. Aigoo! Aigoo!"

It is my mother. This is the voice of my mother.

A loud bellow erupts out of her. Out of me.

Seismic howls, wails, fill my apartment. The walls will crumble. Windows, anything glass will surely shatter. I will crack in two. A person's body is not capable of crying this hard, this loud. My forehead rests on the floor, the telephone, too heavy, beside me.

After some time, Omma has stopped crying. "Anny?" she says in a raspy voice.

"Mother? Omma?"

Again, we break down and sob. I've attempted to sit up my head back against the seat of the armchair. Tears pool in my ears, fall onto the chair cushion. My sinuses plug up. Omma continues to cry. I sit motionless. Spent.

"Anny," she whispers, not trusting her voice. "Anny, my heart hurt so much," she says, her voice quivering. "You go to American, I want to die. Oh, I hurt so much. I cry. For three years I cry."

Once again we give in to tears. Tears will fill my apartment. An ocean will be my home.

When our sobs finally lessen, and I have somewhat composed myself, it comes to me. "You speak English!"

"Oh, sure. I speak-a English. Long time ago Omma talk good English. But Omma no talk English for many, many years. I forget so much English." I tell her I'm impressed, she speaks very well.

"You eat? What you like to eat?" I rattle off some foods, but really, I'll eat anything.

"You like Korean food?"

"Um, sure, a little," I say, but I'm unable to recall the last time I ate Korean food.

"Why you eat only a little Korean food?" She asks. I tell her I have not had that many opportunities to eat it. I only know kimchi and rice.

"Aigoo! I make you Korean food. You come to Korean and I make best Korean food. Aigoo," she says, disappointed. I tell her I'm up for that.

"Anny, Omma have bad luck, so much bad luck. What ya gonna do? But I never forget you. Never. Everyday I think about you. You marry? Why no marry? But you have to marry some day, you want have children. No? Everybody want children. You have boyfriend?

No boyfriend? Why no boyfriend? Omma no like men. Too much trouble. So much trouble. What you do for money? Restaurant jobi? Ah, no good! Aigoo! Why you work in restaurant?" I explain it is only temporary, that some day I'll find a career.

"You college girl? Good, good! You have good education. Omma want you have good education. I send you to American to go to school." I assure her I did get a good education.

"You go to church? I want you have churchman for father. He good man? Your mother good, too? Good, good. Why you no have office jobi? Anny, you work in office. You marry. Find good husband."

"Uh, we'll see," I say, although nothing she suggests interests me.

"How old you, Anny? Twenty-nine? Ack, soon you too old to marry."

I am a bit surprised by her archaic thinking. "I am not too old to get married! *If* I choose to marry."

"You marry soon, okay? What life you have if you no marry? You eat? I think you don't eat. Why no eat?" I explain that I'm trying to lose a little weight.

"You fat? You no fat. I think you like Omma. Young girl time, Omma never fat. Okay. Take it easy, huh? You eat something."

I have just talked to my mother. The mother who gave me away twenty-three years ago. The mother I have not seen since I was almost seven. I just talked to my mother! We said so much, well, actually she did, as if she needed to get it all in on our first conversation.

I crawl into bed and sleep, expecting to find when I wake that it was all a dream.

⸺⁀⸺

It is our second conversation, and Omma wants to know if she should call me Anny or Kate. She is matter-of-fact about the name change, not saddened like Oppa when I tell her my sister's name and Anny are too similar. But she's confused as to what to call me.

"I call you Anny? No problem this," Omma says. She is pleased. I tell her I learned my full name when I became an American citizen at ten.

"You American girl, that's good."

"Yah, but the funny part was I didn't spell my name correctly when I signed my citizenship papers."

I missed half a day of school, my afternoon music class, where we were learning to play *Mary Has A Little Lamb* on the recorder. Instead, I went to the courthouse to become an American citizen. It was an important day.

When mom and dad first told me, I was scared. What would they make me do? My parents weren't sure. They thought I'd get a flag and I'd probably talk to a judge. Why did I have to talk to a judge? My parents were only guessing; they were uncertain too.

I did get a flag and it sat on my bookshelf next to Sebastian so he could enjoy it too. I did talk to the judge, but I don't remember what he said. I nodded yes whenever I thought I should.

What would I remember about this monumental occasion? That I did not know my first name was Catherine. And I did not know how to spell Catherine. I was supposed to write my full name, which I did: Katie Strand. Except it turned out my full name was Catherine Anne Strand.

When mom saw I had written Katie on the official document she explained my first name was Catherine.

"No, it isn't. My name is Katie."

"That's your nickname."

"What's a nickname?" She explains it's a shorter form of a longer name.

"Why do I have two names then?" One was my official name and the other was informal, casual, therefore a nickname.

"How do you spell Catherine? Mom spelled it out. "Why does it start with a C and not a K like Katie?" Mom has always liked the spelling of Catherine with a C.

"Then why isn't Katie spelled with a C?" She didn't like Katie spelled with a C, besides, it was just a nickname.

"Aigoo!" Omma says, when I tell her this story, "Omma call you Anny."

She is pleased, however, that my parents kept some semblance of my original name.

⸺ↄ⸺

A few days later Omma calls. She says she will call from her house now that she is back in Ansan. I can telephone her there any time too. She asks me if I still wear my *hanbok,* my traditional Korean dress she sent with me to my new life.

"Do I still wear it? It doesn't exactly fit me anymore...."

Was it the language barrier? Did she mean to say *wore,* as in the past tense? As in, wore the dress when I was six? She laughs in confusion, in embarrassment. She did mean *now,* do I wear it now, currently at twenty-nine, with my adult body that cannot possibly squeeze into the dress I wore when I was a child?

We seem to understand at the same moment her state of mind. She is stuck in time, in the past. She still sees me as six-year-old Anny. Her memories still live in the moments before I left. Even though she is talking to the twenty-nine-year-old Anny, her mind has not made the leap to me as an adult.

"No, but I still have it," I assure her. I keep my hanbok, the underskirt, thick cotton socks and blue rubber shoes, along with the red tennis shoes I wore to Minnesota in a box in a closet at my parent's house. I learned that Korean women and girls wear *hanbok* only for special occasions like the Chinese New Year, fall harvest festival or when paying respect to ancestors at ancestral grounds.

Omma laughs with pleasure at my story of wearing my hanbok for show and tell in first grade. She says everybody likes hanboks, that maybe when I come to Korea she will have one made for me.

"You bring back to Minnesota and wear for New Year."

"Uh...maybe." But really, I can't see myself wearing the traditional dress as I bar hop in Uptown or downtown Minneapolis on New Year's Eve.

I do not add that my mom could not get all the mud stains out of the hanbok after bringing it to school for show and tell. I dropped it on the school bus during a rain shower.

⎯⎯᠖⎯⎯

Omma continues to stress her concern over my single status. I explain that in America, twenty-nine years old does not mean spinsterhood. I am still young. She is unconvinced I'm in the prime of life. To her way of thinking, I am nearly unmarriable, followed by barren. She also cannot understand my doubt in wanting to have children.

I hesitate to divulge to her my most significant, meaningful relationship. The man I thought I would marry.

⎯⎯᠖⎯⎯

Nine months after graduating from college, at twenty-five, after putting a year and a half into special education courses, then switching to elementary education courses, ("You teacher, good, Anny!") and transferring to a Minnesota college, I decided teaching was not what I wanted to do. Instead, I majored in Mass Communications, with an emphasis in advertising.

Ben was a creative director for a major advertising agency. He was intelligent, funny and adventurous. He walked an interesting path with one foot still in pseudo hippie living and the other in yuppie land.

We met at a yuppie bar a few weeks after the Twins won the 1987 World Series, the city still on a high from its historic win. I was out celebrating my birthday with friends. I saw him from across the bar. I could not decide if he looked more like Dan Gladden, the Twin's first baseman I had a crush on at the time, or Robert Redford with his strawberryblondhair and firm jaw.

He noticed me noticing him. That night he built a fire at his place, we talked and shared stories of our lives, and I spent the night. The next day a dozen red roses arrived at the house I was renting with two other girls. In March, after asking him if I could live with him temporarily, I had plans to backpack in Europe that summer. I moved in and stayed for two years.

We camped and cross-country skied up north. Portaged a section of the Boundary Waters. I got my scuba diving certification in Mexico on a two-week trip specifically so I could dive with him in Mexico and Belize. Ben bought a house and I painted most of the rooms, hung window blinds with a screwdriver and a strong wrist, no power tools for me! I stained a dining room table and six chairs. I made it home for a time.

Meanwhile, he waited for me to find myself. I was indecisive as to what I wanted out of life. He hoped I had higher aspirations than waitressing, but only after getting fired at the restaurant did I make a job change. I liked staying out late and sleeping in during the day. While

I was not a flirt, the attention I'd receive from men bothered him. An evening out with an ex-boyfriend did not sit well with him. It seemed he did not care for my wandering ways, my laissez faire attitude.

But when I said I thought I was ready for marriage, he laughed. He didn't think I was anywhere near ready. In my mind, I made myself vulnerable; his laughter, like a serrated knife, sawed at the core of my worst fear. Rejection.

Our relationship fell into a rut, a daily grind of domesticity and routine. A death knell for a girl yearning for adventure, spontaneity, too willing to take flight if life became stagnant, if she felt unwanted. A girl who had no idea how to be a partner, who used sex as power, and an escape, who shielded herself from rejection, avoided the scourge of abandonment at all cost. A belief that I held surfaced: I was not good enough.

About a year and a half into my relationship with Ben, I met Gorgeous. I was sitting at an outdoor coffee shop before going to work at a local newspaper where I sold advertising space, enjoying a currant and buttermilk scone and a latte, engrossed in reading a newspaper, that I did not notice him as he stood at my table.

He cleared his throat to get my attention, introduced himself, and asked if he could sit with me. *Are there no more seats?* was my thought, only to realize we were the only two on the patio.

One look at him and I became dumb with desire. I wanted him. I had to have him. I had never felt that way about a man. He was Gorgeous. Tall. Masculine. Sensual full lips, strong jaw, largedarkblueeyes. For once I had trouble maintaining my I-can-take-or-leave-you demeanor. We talked briefly. But we took each other in. He told me later he had seen me there the week before, had wanted to stop but he would have been late for a meeting. Every morning he drove by hoping he'd find me there. He gave me his business card; I gave him mine. We talked every day until the weekend when we met for dinner. I am sure I told Ben I was meeting a girlfriend.

The physical attraction was overpowering. I could not concentrate on our conversation during dinner. Darkblueeyes surrounded by long lashes gazed at me with open desire. His full lower lip begged to be sucked. I wanted his mouth devouring every inch of me. My fingers tingled to pull on his darkbrownwavy hair. Thoughts of wrapping my legs around his lean hips left me dizzy. To lick, to bite his six-pack belly was soon to become my temple of worship. I could not get enough of his toned body. After hours of mauling each other we fell asleep. At three in the morning, I awoke in a panic. Ben would wonder where I was.

On the day I moved out, three months later, Ben drew me a hot bath. After a leisurely soak, I dressed and spent extra time on my make up. I was going with Gorgeous to a launch party at a music producer's studio. The company he owned installed sound systems; one of his clients had a studio out in the suburbs.

Ben made a dinner of grilled salmon and fettucine in alfredo sauce. We cried more than we ate. While I knew I was hurting him, I was sad and excited. Gorgeous offered excitement, something new. I was immature, unsettled, grasping for something beyond, something *out there*. I just knew Gorgeous was the answer to my wandering.

Our seven month "relationship" became an excuse for all-day sex. We had nothing in common but our mutual attraction for each other's bodies. He stayed fit by training for triathlons. I stayed fit by running and having sex with him. There were no boundaries for our sexual antics. We had no shame. In private. In public. On a four hour drive to his friend's cabin, I wanted to have sex with him while he drove. After weaving in and out of traffic getting his jeans down, adjusting his seat to fit me between him and the steering wheel, it wasn't as exciting as the idea of it. The highlight was a trucker driving along side us honking and encouraging us on. The couple we stayed with wanted to have sex with us. As much as I was intrigued with the idea of group sex, I couldn't get enough of him; I did not want to divide my attention on others. He could not agree more.

But, then, inexplicably, he disappeared for days. At some point I realized he was addicted to smoking pot. The first time he did not show up the entire weekend, I was out of my mind with confusion. My remedy was to call a girlfriend, meet for cocktails and proceed to analyze the entire scenario in minute detail, in hopes of gleaning insight into his behavior. She concluded I needed to dump him and move on. It so happened our waiter was an adorable young Irish lad. What better way to move on from my troubles than with a new prospect? I agreed to go listen to music with him the following night. But the next night Gorgeous showed up at my door an hour before I was to meet the waiter. The telephone rang incessantly, as Gorgeous and I made up. I knew it was the Irish boy wondering where I was. I never called him back.

The second time Gorgeous did not show up, I called my friend Mark, upset and needing to be consoled. He comforted me, reminding me how out of control I felt the last time this had happened. Gorgeous' erratic behavior and lack of follow-through butted up against my fear of abandonment. I did not like being left, ignored, phone calls unanswered. He was stepping into my behavior territory. He was older, he should behave better. Our sex life began waning, too.

It was time to move on. Except there was no one waiting in the wings, no boy or man to distract me from myself. I had hurt Ben, the one good man in my life. With loneliness gnawing at me, I was tempted to crawl back to him, but I respected him enough to stay away. I owed him that much.

7

Korea Social Service Inc., February 13, 1969
<u>Description of Child:</u>
No particular problem, habit or behavior has been found on her yet. In the worker's opinion, the present growth and development of Anny certainly seems to be normal for her age, it is convinced that she will be capable in making adequate adjustment to any substitute home.

July 1991

"Your sparkle is gone," my adoptive mom said to me over Vietnamese eggrolls, months before the phone call of my Korean family's search for me. We were having lunch at a popular Vietnamese restaurant. It turned out to be a place we both liked. "You aren't yourself. Your eyes...they don't look right. What do you need? What can I do?" She had called a number of times in early summer, left messages asking if I was doing all right. I knew I wasn't. But I figured it would pass. My gung-ho attitude was gone, replaced, she said, by listlessness and disinterest.

I was surprised by my mom's invitation to get together. She and I did not meet for breakfast, lunch, or dinner. We didn't shop together. We kept each other at arm's length as far back as I could remember. I was not used to her attention, nor did I know how to answer her questions. I did not know how to reply to her concerns.

What was my problem? I usually bounced back from any situation, but I found I no longer could. My travel plans stalled. I was unable to pull out of my dispirited funk. A concerned friend suggested I see a therapist.

This therapist seemed to think I was depressed. I agreed. I was. He suggested that my depression had something to do with being adopted. *Adopted?* Where did that come from? My adoption had nothing to do with what I was going through. That happened long ago. I was not about to dwell in the past, especially when I had a future to think about. I pooh-poohed his psychology. I was twenty-eight years old. I was depressed because I didn't know what to do with my life. After graduating from college, I assumed I'd find a meaningful job, but that was not the trajectory my life had taken. I started waitressing with the intention of earning enough money to travel and work abroad for a year or so. Then I would come back and get a real job.

The famous expression, *those who wander are not necessarily lost,* did not sum up my situation, was not my motto. Mine was, *I am lost, so I shall wander, escape to other lands,* which was where I turned when roads led to dead ends.

I was caught up in a cycle of drinking and sex and living on tips. I felt like a failure. I come from Korean stock and a Swedish upbringing, which if I were to believe the stereotypes of these ethnic groups, means hard worker, one who toils endlessly, which I had done up to that point.

But he continued to badger me about my adoption. How did I feel about being adopted? *How did I feel about it?* That was history. I was here so he could get me on track. Help me grab onto a future, not rehash the past. Clearly, he was missing the issue.

His probings and inquiries into my biological mother frustrated me: *How did I feel about her? Was I angry with her?* I didn't remember her. I didn't think about her. She gave me up. She did not get to take up any room in my head. He wondered about my relationship with my adopted parents. With my siblings. With the birth order both bio-logical and within my adoptive family. *What did that have to do with it?* He believed that the order in which one was born could affect the new family dynamics. I thought I was probably the oldest in Korea, had had a younger brother who was adopted before me. In my adop-tive family, though Tim and I were the same age, I was the second oldest, his birthday was a few months after mine.

The therapist was of little help. Or so I thought. I was seeking direc-tion for my future; I was desperate to move forward; he thought in order to do so I needed to come to terms with my childhood. I wanted a quick fix; he claimed there wasn't one.

I was ready to quit the counseling sessions when he asked me why I was hell bent on refusing to discuss my adoption. Why was I in denial of my Korean heritage? While I remained silent and annoyed, he shared his findings in working with adoptees. If adoptees acknowl-edged their adoption, inquired about their heritage, connected with other adoptees, and received support by their adoptive family, both through immersion of the culture and healthy discussions on the sub-ject, by their teens, they transitioned into adulthood more confident in managing their lives. If, however, adoptees chose to forsake their heritage, he found many became depressed in their late twenties and struggled to find a footing for themselves.

That was my playbook. The story of my life. I realized there was truth to what he said. It was unnerving, as if he had watched the mov-ie of my life of denial: of my heritage, of my culture, my adoption. I had altered myself as best I could to the image I believed I needed to make it in this culture and within my adoptive family.

As if he hadn't given me enough to chew on, the therapist con-tinued. Depression is a manifestation of anger turned inward. Of that I had no doubt. No doubt. Wasn't I the hot head who did not hesitate to quit a job, walked out several times if I felt mistreated? Who got fired twice in one year for disagreeing with my employer's policies? Who went on a kicking tantrum on a man's headlight when he parked behind me, bumped my car as I was getting out, and was incensed when he feigned indifference, did not apologize? I shouted obscenities at him while trying my damndest to at least crack his headlight.

―∽―

The fights throughout my childhood with my sister.

No matter what the fight was about, it seemed I was in the wrong. Never mind AnnMarie got gum in my hair, *Why such a fuss, turpentine will get that out.* Which it did not. *It's just a haircut. If you continue carrying on like this, then you can go to your room.* My beautiful long hair had to be cut to my shoulders. *Do you have to make a mountain out of a molehill? She returned your sweater, didn't she? No, she should not have taken your journal. She said she didn't read it. We're done talking about this. All right, young lady, now you're pushing it, up to your room.*

Feeling powerless, I lashed out at my sister, yelled and screamed at her. In turn, she gave me the silent treatment, willfully ignored me. She'd stand immobile, fixed on some object to the left, right of my face. Her unwillingness to regard my feelings, to acknowledge my existence, enraged me. I slapped her. One time I went so far as to take the riding trophies and ribbons she'd won in horse show competitions and threw them out her upstairs bedroom window. My parents sent me to my room. AnnMarie was consoled. The neverending cycle of conflict without learning how to resolve our battles, cemented.

―∽―

I understood I was to be my sister's friend and protector. If I did not include her when I played with my friends, mom got upset with me. At a family reunion, my cousin, who was AnnMarie's age, wanted my attention, to play badminton with me. I tried to involve my sister, but with three players it was awkward. No matter how much I tried to explain to my mom, *she didn't want to play with us,* mom's repeated line, *Family first. Your family comes first, Katie,* told me I had once again disappointed her.

The summer my friend, Debbie and I were twelve we went to a Lutheran camp. AnnMarie came too. At camp, I made friends easily and was constantly surrounded by my peers. Because of our age difference, AnnMarie and I were in different cabins; I rarely saw her. But I heard from friends that a girl was bothering her. I was incensed. *No one picks on my sister.* I was on my way to play Capture the Flag with a small army of friends when we decided to confront the girl before the game. We did not have a plan nor did I know what I'd say to make her stop harassing my sister.

As I approached the bully, a younger boy who liked our company, ran up to me excited to show the garter snake he found. Snakes frightened me witless. Every time we saw one at the cabin, I'd shake with fright right after screaming loudly. I had refused to touch the ones Tim and Peter found.

But without thinking, I grabbed the snake out of his hand, and ran to the mean girl standing nearby. I called out her name, and as she turned in my direction, I flung the snake at her. I thought *I* screamed when seeing a snake! I guess it's extra frightening to have it thrown in your face. I yelled at her to leave my sister alone or next time she'd find a snake in her sleeping bag. She never did come near my sister.

One summer, while my maternal grandparents were visiting from Texas, as they often did, grandpa came upon my sister and I playing checkers. I was probably about ten or eleven, AnnMarie, seven or eight. My brothers were rooting us on. It was the critical point of the game, where no matter which way my sister moved, I could jump her pieces with my kinged checkers and come out winning. AnnMarie pondered her no-win situation in hopes of some unforeseen strategy yet uncovered, ignoring Tim and Peter's repeated chants, *you're finished* and *it's over.*

Grandpa came into the living room and silently observed the checkerboard. "Look kids," he said as he pointed out the living room window, "look at the pretty blue jay." Sure enough, a blue jay was standing on top of the bushes as if he too wanted in on the game. The four of us ran over to the window exclaiming what a beauty it was and the good luck it probably represented. With a quick flap of its cerulean wings, the bird flew away, most likely from our loud proclamations over his beauty. My mind focused back on the game. Victory was mine. It was a formality, really, but I did enjoy jumping my sister's checkers.

Looking down at the checkerboard, I noticed something was different. Was it my imagination or were the checker pieces on different squares? Upon closer examination, AnnMarie, too, saw that, indeed, she could move and even jump my kings—to win.

At first, none of us could imagine how I had missed these obvious moves…. I think we realized it at the same moment. The unfathomable. Had Grandpa switched the pieces? I dared not look at the others for fear their faces would reveal what I was beginning to wonder.

Like a pinball, my head, zinged and pinged with questions. Did he switch the checker pieces? Why would he do that? What did that mean? Did he want AnnMarie to win? Did he rig the pieces so I would lose? Why? Why? My face flushed with shame and uncertainty.

We half-heartedly finished the game. I looked on as my sister jumped my crowned pieces to win. Silently we folded up the board, packed away the red and black checkers.

Did we ever talk about this incident? No. If we talked about it then it meant it really happened. If we did not mention it, we could, instead, doubt our own eyes and memory. Maybe grandpa really hadn't moved the pieces. Maybe none of us saw the winning checker moves until we stepped away and only then saw the possibilities of my averted win.

We had learned the benefits of stepping away to get a better perspective from working on jigsaw puzzles up at the cabin, where our impatience grew the longer we sat staring at the puzzle, making it difficult to find connecting pieces. We'd take a break, find something else to do, came back with fresh eyes, and was often rewarded, finding pieces easily for a spell.

But this was not like the jigsaw puzzles. There were four sets of eyes on the board and a limited number of checkers left. It was not a complicated board. But then we had to reconcile what it meant if grandpa switched the pieces. Unless we did not talk about it. Yes! That is what we'll do. We will not talk about it. We will not think about it. It's unpleasant and it makes us uncomfortable. If we do not let it out into the light, we cannot see it. It will be as if it never happened.

―◦

Much to my parent's annoyance, I gabbed endlessly with PeggyDebbieDeanneScottLoriJim. My parents tired of fielding my calls, exasperated at tripping over me as I lounged on the wooden phone bench, feet propped up on the side of the refrigerator in the high traffic area between kitchen and upstairs. They imposed a five-minute limit on the telephone. *Dad's parishioners might call. No one needs to talk that long, that often.*

Through their silence, my parents, especially my mom, discouraged me from drawing attention to myself. Never mind my face ensured the unlikelihood of this during my childhood, but my temperament played a role as well. My enthusiasm seemed to know no bounds. With numerous friends, a sunny disposition, a sense of humor, an Asian face that people eventually deemed cute, even pretty, I was social and outgoing, which was always pointed out in my report card. *Too social. She needs improvement in the visiting area.* My teachers insisted I rein it in which I did not do, at least not until high school.

But in other ways, I complied. I wanted my parent's approval though I did not know how to go about securing it. Once, I explained with the full-throttled enthusiasm of a nine-year-old, that when I grew up I would be a writer. I had just penned a story I could not wait to read to mom. The main character was a rich girl who lived in a mansion by an ocean. She was relieved to be an only child for she recognized the downside of siblings, sisters in particular, from her friends who had too many of them. How relieved she was not to have a sister who took things, listened in on phone conversations, mooned over her boyfriend. But one look at mom's sour face stopped me mid sentence. I mumbled it was just a dumb story, didn't like it much myself. As mom walked away, I closed my notebook for good.

Decades later I would fully understand and admit what place I held in the family hierarchy. But I began to sense what my role in the family was by the time I was in junior high. During those years, I was on the swim team and at a home swim meet, I happened to glance up at the balcony to see mom, dad, and AnnMarie walk in. I was taken by surprise. No one from my family came to my meets, or to my softball, flag football or basketball games.

That moment, I was to compete in my strongest event, the front crawl. My coach was confident with my ability in this stroke. I had won many times before. I had this. But seeing my parents, my sister, flipped a switch. It began in my stomach. The whistle blew. I dove in. It was as though I was slogging through split pea soup. My arms and legs churned, beat the water, but I could not move at my usual speed. I labored to finish. I came in almost last in my best event.

⸻

My sophomore year of high school, we moved into a newly built house in Minnetonka. My parents were the first to pick out a lot in a new development where they designed and built their dream house. It turned into an exclusive area for presidents and vice presidents of large companies, a television anchor personality, a football player, and other wealthy families resided.

The neighborhood was filled with Porsches, Jaguars, and big boats. We were the neighbors who instead drove a junky Javelin one summer, a rusty Gremlin another. These were the cars dad purchased for his children's summer jobs. These were the cars that sat out in the driveway.

Furthermore, a garage door was a luxury dad did without. His favorite joke was to claim he didn't need an automatic garage door opener, he had five of them: mom, Peter, me, Tim and AnnMarie. He did not tire of that joke.

Months after settling in to our house, Cathy moved in next door. If it was unfortunate to start at a new school as a sophomore, as I did, it was worse for Cathy, a junior. While we became friends by proximity, for a while we had enough in common to develop a friendship.

As a token of gratitude for befriending their daughter, her parents invited me to vacation with them in the Florida Keys over spring break.

It was the first time anyone thanked me in such a generous way for something that came pretty easily to me. I was excited by the idea of a vacation in an exotic location. I paid for my airfare from my waitress tips (I worked throughout high school), Cathy's parents paid for the rest of the trip.

We stayed in a timeshare condominium on Key Largo with a large outdoor pool where Cathy, her sister, Shelly, and I spent as much time as we could. I had bought what I considered to be the most beautiful two-piece string bikini, and I was going to get my money's worth from it. The suit was burnt orange with a dark brown floral pattern, and after no more than twenty minutes in the sun, my chocolate colored skin matched the brown print.

On one of our first days, we met Tommy at the pool. He was also staying in the condo with his family. He drove down from Orlando in his silver Cadillac convertible. A high school girl could not dream up anything better than this set up.

Cathy's parents treated us to a day of deep-sea fishing. Her dad hired a guide and his assistant to take all of us to catch fish and dive for conch. The guide's assistant, Donut, was nicknamed this presumably because he liked donuts. I don't think he spoke the entire four hours we were together.

Our guide was an older man with a leathery tan and white hair, who constantly joked and played tricks on us. Because of his jovial nature, Cathy and I decided to call him Grandpa, especially after I caught my first grunt fish. I firmly believed it was Grandpa making the odd noises though he insisted the grunt sound was coming from the fish. I accused him of pulling our leg. I mean, really, I had never heard fish make noise of any sort and I was not about to believe it from a prankster.

Grandpa would bring the fish close to me, and I thought the sound was louder than the previous, proving to me that it was Grandpa. Each time, I'd startle, jump a foot upward and scamper away. Grandpa thought that was worth seeing over and over.

He dove for conch and tried to convince us the transparent tube shaped piece from the recesses of the conch was a delicacy. He would pop the thing whole in his mouth and laugh as we squealed in disgust. None of us were willing to eat it raw.

After the fishing excursion Cathy and I sat in the shade of a palm tree and whined. Our sunburned bodies pulsed with heat, the sun having a good laugh at our vain attempts at using sun block. My shoulders were burnt; it was painful to move my arms, making it difficult to dress. I put on a loose-fitting, lavender colored linen blouse. Cathy had to button the three large brown buttons; I could not bend my arms to do it myself.

That evening when the cool air blew through the island, Cathy realized she had forgotten her sweatshirt on Grandpa's boat. We had plans to go out with Tommy that night to ride around in his convertible, but first we'd stop at Grandpa's place and retrieve her sweatshirt. There was nothing better to a high school girl than driving around in a convertible with a nice guy, your friend, and a night sky filled with billions of stars to light your way to remind you how lucky you are. We cranked up the volume to Pat Benatar singing, *Hit Me With Your Best Shot*, and sang with abandon.

Every light was on at Grandpa's house. He was happy to see us. He invited us in to his living room, with books piled everywhere, on the couch, armchair, and round coffee table. After explaining why we'd come, he had Donut fetch Cathy's sweatshirt. He asked why was I holding my arms out stiffly from my body. Bad sunburn was my explanation. He offered to put some lotion on me. I had just applied some aloe before leaving and I was fine. He insisted. I thanked him and assured him I would be all right.

Donut returned with the sweatshirt. We heard Queen's *We Will Rock You* blaring in the other room. Tommy asked about the album. Donut invited us into his room to check out his vinyl record collection. As we headed in, Grandpa caught my hand and led me to the couch, offering the bottle of lotion. Telling him again that I was fine did not stop him from putting some on my forearm. Indeed, it felt cool on my hot skin. He continued to rub the lotion over my arms as he touted the benefits of this particular brand of lotion over the others.

He guided me onto my back. He touched my stomach, said how soothing the lotion would be. He talked on and on, but I stopped listening. My brain was trying to make sense of what was happening. Something wasn't right, what he was doing. *But this man is like a Grandpa to us, we call him Grandpa, he took us fishing, he's our friend, he's an adult, he'll stop soon.* These thoughts, like a record, repeated, looped, and skipped in my brain. At some point he had my shorts unzipped and his fingers were caressing me. Murmurs. Words. Dirty words. My mind froze. I think I left my body.

What snapped me out of it? Did he make a sudden move? Was he attempting to take off my shorts? I leapt from the couch, pulled up my shorts, and as I ran for the door, I yelled to Cathy and Tommy to follow me. I ran as fast as I could to the car, jumped in the backseat, and started to cry. I waited. And waited. Didn't they hear my screams and the urgency in my voice? I realized they had not; not with Donut's stereo cranked to high decibels.

I ran back to the house. Burst through the front door. Cathy. On the couch. Grandpa...doing...to...her...what...he...did...to me. Her face was my face. A girl dazed. Her brain frozen, unable to comprehend what was being done to her, could not register it, the man we had befriended, had fun with just hours before.

I cried out. *Get up. Get up.* I ran to the other room. Screamed to Tommy. Ran to the car. What was taking so long? I waited. Waited. Finally, once in the car, Tommy squealed out of the gravel driveway on two wheels.

We rode in silence. The open convertible flew down the highway faster than when we started out. I was cold. I tried to process what had happened to us. I thought about what could have happened.

Tommy parked in the back parking lot of the condo. None of us moved.

"We have to tell your parents," I said in a calm voice. "We have to call the police."

Cathy protested. We didn't need to tell her parents. It was late. They wouldn't be happy to be woken up so late.

"Well, I'm not happy with what he did to us," I said, not so calmly this time.

We went around and around on whether to tell her parents. I was angry with this old man for betraying our trust. I was angry with him for touching us, thinking he could do what he did to us. And I was angry with myself for letting it happen.

"If he could do what he did to us," I said, "what would stop him from doing this to other girls?" This was probably not his first time touching girls. I was not versed, had not learned the language for what he had done—*sexual assault.*

It was early morning before we could agree to wake Cathy's parents. The police came and took our report. I told them I wanted to bring charges against him. I wanted to take this man to court and I wanted him in jail. The adults convinced me that on a practical level this would not be in my best interest. Who knew how many times I might have to come down here and deal with all the legal wranglings. The police assured me that with our report, if he tried to do this to another person they would have enough on him to bring him to court. I wanted to believe them.

It was particularly upsetting to hear he was a retired judge.

When I came home and told mom about this incident, she was washing dishes and cleaning up the kitchen. Although she was startled, she never let go of the dishcloth. Washing dishes. Wiping counters. Kitchen spotless. I waited for her to do and say more than the exclamatory, *That's terrible!*

I sat at the kitchen table. Watched mom complete her tasks. It was important to have a clean and functioning kitchen at all times.

───⑤───

There is a photograph of me standing in my aunt and uncle's backyard along with all my cousins, brothers and sister, when I was about twelve or thirteen years old. My long hair is pulled back in a red and blue embroidered headband, and I have on what is suppose to be a long sleeved white turtleneck, except it's too short, too tight through the upper arms. Over that I wear a classic 1970's red knit vest, which accentuates my protruding stomach.

I was an active kid, and thanks to Title IX, I was involved in every sport that was offered during my pre-teen years: softball, soccer, flag football, swim team, and basketball. I also loved riding my second-hand, three-speed bike that dad found in the want ads.

So how did I get so round if I was active? By having seconds of everything during dinner regardless of whether I was full or not. Another scoop of Hungarian goulash, though I liked it not, same for the bland ground beef chili, flavorless without the chili powder, too spicy for my dad, was served on the side. My dinner plate had to be filled twice in order for me to feel I had eaten enough. That day at my relative's house, I filled my plate to almost overflowing with pasta, sauce and parmesan cheese, both times.

I never had enough. I needed to feel the full weight of food in my belly to stave off my fears and insecurities. I wanted to fit in. I did not want to be the girl that stood out because she looked like no one else in the community. I wanted to be part of the majority where I could take my existence for granted, where I had no doubt of my place in the world.

I found ways to fill up my yearnings and fears and a growing sense of loneliness. If I could feel stuffed on the inside with food, then there was no room for the other emotions. I found gratification where I could: in the refrigerator and in cupboards. There I would rummage looking to stifle the emptiness. For me, that first plate was to nourish my body, but I still felt hollow. There was never solace in that last forkful. A second plateful of chicken, rolls, potatoes would help to numb, deaden those feelings.

During my junior year in high school, after a spring break vacation in Mazatlan, Mexico with my Spanish class, I discovered how to control my weight.

The purpose of going to a Spanish speaking country was to learn Spanish. For me, it turned out to be for the beaches and the food. In various tourist-designated restaurants, my young palate discovered dinner rolls slathered with as much unsalted butter as I wanted. While my friends daintily took a bite or two of their rolls, I consumed three or four at a sitting. I looked forward to each meal; even for breakfast, rolls were plentiful.

By the end of our week long vacation I thought I had gained weight, which was confirmed by a photograph someone took of my friend, Sandra and I on our last morning. She looked adorable with her short auburn hair framing her smiling face, her trendy light blue preppy shirt, dark khakis still fitting comfortably on her slim frame.

I, too, wore blue khakis, except my thighs were stuffed in mine. The pockets accentuated my hips hitting them where the five pounds of bread had settled in the widest part of my body. The buttons on my pink preppy shirt gaped open. My belly stuck out.

When I came home, I was horrified to discover none of my clothes fit comfortably. During a free block at school, I ran into a friend and we reminisced over our magical spring break, exchanging stories of our escapades, especially the ease we had at dodging the adults, our chaperones. I began to complain about the weight I gained. My friend looked at me blankly. She was as slim as ever. If I thought about it, all the girls on the trip remained slim except for me. How was that possible? She shared the ways one could stave off weight gain.

One friend was anorexic. Her beautifully proportioned body whittled down to less than a hundred pounds. She looked frail, a wisp of her former self. I had not seen her in some time, but one spring day, our senior year, I sat with her during lunch. She tried to eat a pear yet I saw how difficult it was for her, the anxiety obvious on her hollow face.

In contrast, I was fixated on food, continued to gain weight, alternating with dieting and eating as little as possible. A friend and I would head over to Perkins, order hamburgers and fries, carrot cake for dessert. We stopped on the way home at a health food store to buy carob covered almonds; we heard carob was good for us.

I attempted the Scarsdale diet; only cottage cheese for me. I fasted. Feeling deprived, I ate before my shift, during my shift and afterward at the restaurant where I worked. None of it involved anything healthy. At times I went through McDonald's drive-thru, too embarrassed to go in to order, parked on some side street, and consumed a Big Mac, apple pie, and shake. Threw the garbage out the window. I did not want to bring home any evidence of my out-of-control eating.

I became a closet eater. I made sure no one saw my multiple clandestine trips into the kitchen to eat small pieces of chocolate cake far into the night.

At last I found a way to stop gaining weight, by bingeing and purging. I hated to make myself throw up, always feeling exhausted afterwards.

But any time I felt especially lonely or scared, I was quick to seek out an overabundance of food. As Holly Golightly said, she went to Tiffany's when the mean reds came out. I over ate, over indulged, obsessed over food when my mean reds appeared. Laxatives also became another way to keep the weight down.

I did not give much thought to that night in Florida with Grandpa. There were no discussions with my parents over this incident. It was another unfortunate occurrence that needed to be swept under the rug, to be forgotten. I would not realize it had left its mark on me until I was older. Over the years I learned to bury unresolved issues, feelings of anger, frustration, powerlessness. Disconnected and adrift from my family, the community where I lived, I could not navigate the choppy waters of teen life.

8

It was a half-hearted decision to attend college, much less a college in Texas. My first choice was to not follow the traditional educational path. I itched to travel and see other continents, meet people from various parts of the world. Wasn't that an education in its own right? But college was the avenue my parent's valued. A Lutheran college was also a must since I would get some financial assistance. So I believed a Lutheran college in California was the place for me. Mom and dad thought otherwise. Without coming right out and saying so, I understood their concern was that I might take to the beach life, and other shenanigans I could not yet imagine. A cousin, whom my parents respected, touted the warm climate and the Olympic size pool at his college in Texas. Warm and pool won me over.

Many people at the small college were baffled by my appearance. *What is she anyway,* the boys asked my friends. People mostly did not see me; I was invisible to them, like beige wallpaper. Or if I was seen, it was negative attention.

I was a waitress at an off-campus eatery a few nights a week. It was here I became astute at reading the body language of customers I waited on. These patrons, usually locals or from neighboring towns, sometimes got mighty quiet when I approached the table, shifted in their chairs, made no eye contact, barely moved their mouths to give me their order, as if expending any amount of energy was an acknowledgment of my existence. They did not want me waiting on them. It couldn't be *me*, per se, since they didn't know me, I reminded myself. Some became irritated or down right upset at my presence. Others even complained to Randy, the manager, they wanted a different waitress.

Randy was gay and had his own experience of offending people because of his sexual preference. His wry, satirical humor made him a favorite among the employees. But when faced with verbal, physical acts of prejudice, he showed no tolerance. If customers complained about me, he saw through their guise. He knew it was not my waitressing abilities that bothered them. He flat out said to those customers that I was their waitress and if they didn't like it they could leave. Some left. Others were wary of me but made do. Others were wary of me and would not make do. They had difficulty placing their drink and dinner order with me, taking longer than usual to order, changing their mind multiple times, my notepad becoming illegible, scratching out their first, second, third selection, which they found humorous.

The first time a customer complained, and left, Randy went on a swearing streak in the back room. *Fucking bastards. Fucking racist pigs.* Lena, a hostess, and Mexican, had an intimate understanding of racial slurs spewed at her, as did Saul the cook; both approved of Randy's colorful words and actions.

I was impressed by Randy's limitless combination of curses but more by his open rejection of bigotry. No one I knew reacted openly. I pretended I did not hear the ugly words, was too preoccupied with looking off in the other direction. But witnessing his reactions, his unwillingness to believe it was not happening began to shape my thinking. He refused to shy away from racism, bigotry, prejudiced words. He called it by name. He consistently made an effort to rebuke and reject changing, diminishing, erasing himself, and others, as the society at large expected he do. That *we minorities* do.

These customers, if they stayed, left no tip. Or else they left a pile of pennies in a glass of water to express their dislike for me. My head and heart raged with fury. *Fuck you, motherfuckers.* Each racial situation pierced me deeply, an emotional internal bleed. To myself, and then to Randy and other understanding employees, I began calling them the Invisible Makers. It had a gentler ring to it than *bigot, racist, motherfucker.*

My Texan boyfriend, Bo, was more open-minded, I thought. We met at his frat party down by the Guadalupe River. Even though I tried to convince him that I couldn't dance the two step he was persistent. He believed he could teach me. After hours of trying he became a believer. I was never successful at learning those darn moves, yet he thought I was okay anyway. It was a relationship in flux. Most of the time we were better off as friends, but by late spring we were hanging out regularly. He wanted me to meet his mother. She offered to take us out to lunch on the last day of finals.

Bo clearly had not told his mother I had a Korean face. I don't think it occurred to either one of us that this might be important information. She was taken aback at the sight of me and did not fully recover.

"Mom, this is Katie."

"Well…why…I'm sure it's nice to meet you. Where you from again? Were you born in Minnesota? (It is at this point, almost always, I know they just want to know *what* I am). Are you an only child? Are they adopted too? Well, now, what were they thinkin' adoptin' a child when they already had their own?"

A few days later, after driving home for the summer in a van with other Minnesota students, Bo called to update me on his mother's impression of me—*yikes,* I thought.

He was happy to report his mom thought I was pretty.

Uh huh…

But, she hoped he wouldn't get serious and want to marry me (what!) because the kids wouldn't look like him. Plus society would have a hard time accepting us.

Bo was matter-of-fact about it, as if her words were not unreasonable, hurtful, *bigoted*. It was not the honesty that bothered me. I, too, was candid with my opinions that rankled others, a departure from Minnesota nice. Though he said he didn't agree with her thinking, I wished he had vehemently opposed his mother's views, set her straight on what his values were, reassured me these were not his beliefs. It occurred to me later that while he might not have agreed in principle, he was complicit by not denouncing, by taking no action. At the time I didn't know how to describe my feelings. I had no language to articulate this exchange, no experience in how to react to these ignorant words.

I went up to my room and cried. I had never been told in such a straightforward manner that because of my face I was problematic to another person. Was it the level of honesty that shook me? In Minnesota, rarely did one openly reveal their prejudice. It was more often a mirage, so subtle, covert, left you second-guessing: *What just happened? Is this what I think it is? Is it just me?*

So what was the problem? Was it her overt beliefs that upset me or the fact that she felt no qualm in stating her prejudiced thoughts to her son? Did others believe these things here in Minnesota?

Mom and Dad wanted to know why I looked glum. When I told them the details of the conversation with Bo's mom, they were upset too.

"I wondered if people would treat you differently," mom said. "This was my concern when you said you wanted to go to school down there. I hoped you wouldn't experience racism or prejudice, that your experience would be different."

I wish she had discussed her concerns with me before I left for college.

I became paranoid. It had been strange to be in a place where I felt invisible. Or stood out and seen as *Foreign*. I began to question my place, living in Minnesota Nice country. Did people in general feel this way towards me, but were unable to say it to my face? If someone was rude to me, was it because they saw me as inferior? How was I to discern whether it was my Asian features or something I did or said that offended?

That a person could be put out by my physical appearance never ceased to surprise me. Never mind that we worshipped the same God, had similar values, lived in the same community, spoke the same language, citizens of the same country. Simply because the make up of my facial features did not mirror theirs, I was less.

I waitressed that summer in Minnesota, at the same restaurant I worked since high school, but now I scrutinized people, suspicious of their motivations. Were they going to stiff me because I had a Korean face? Was the family I was waiting on a clan of racists? I monitored and silently questioned my employer's attitude towards me. Was he giving me fewer hours because he saw me as an Asian girl and they had white employees that must come first?

I was also working as a cashier at a gas station down the road from our house. It was a family-run business, from the grandpa on down to his son and wife. They had a popular deli in the back of the station where you could get the best pastrami on rye. This is where Helmut, the grandpa of the organization, liked to "help out." He came mainly to chat with customers. I always heard laughter coming from the back when he was around. For some reason he liked me. He teased me and I gave it right back. He thought he was catching me off guard with a remark, but I'd come back with a sassy retort that made him laugh. He claimed I had spunk. We enjoyed each other's humor.

It was difficult to believe the world was working against you when time after time, evidence to the contrary proved otherwise. My employers were good to me. I did my jobs well. I genuinely liked people, and mostly people liked me. Between my two jobs where I was dealing with the public, the paranoia I felt was abated for the most part.

That was not to say that I did not experience prejudiced or bigoted behavior. But I learned that if I reassured people who found me suspect that I was a *good* minority, by speaking standard English—no broken English came out of my mouth, proved that I knew their rules, adhered to the conventions, and used proper manners, their concerns were allayed. I did not make them needlessly uncomfortable. *She is an acceptable minority,* was what I hoped they'd believe.

I put it upon myself to represent the model Asian, in particular because I was the *singular* Asian at my high school, in the community. I knew that for many people, I was their first experience of encountering an *Other.* I wanted to make a good impression. Also, it helped to put them at ease by smiling often. I made a practice of doing so after an acquaintance in high school asked why I didn't smile much. I asked her what she meant. *You look mean when you don't smile,* she explained. I did not want to offend, scare anyone away. Soon I went everywhere with a grin on my face.

⸺꘎⸺

I met Patrick the first summer home from college. We did not have much in common. He was a staunch Republican, I, a proud bleeding heart liberal. He was vehemently anti-abortion. I believed a woman should determine what was best for her body. We argued this point countless times. Then I became pregnant.

He was quick to suggest an abortion.

After the abortion, I needed and wanted to be held. Comforted while I cried. He was incapable of offering or giving that kind of support; instead, he was angry because I did not feel up to watching his friend's baseball game after the procedure. I didn't know how to ask for what I needed. I went to my room and slept.

At first, his put downs and belittling remarks were far and few. The first time he said something mean, I threw a glass of beer in his face. I walked out on him in bars and restaurants. What did I know about love at nineteen? I thought my feelings of contempt, irritation, and a roaming eye were all part of what a relationship went through. Weren't we just ironing out the kinks, the bugs?

On a typical night at his parent's house, after indulging on pizza, we sat on the couch wondering what to do with the rest of the evening. Out of nowhere, he asked if I knew why Asian people were referred to as frogs.

"I didn't know they were," (and by whom?).

"They are. It's because their eyes bulge out like frog's eyes." Without missing a beat he asked if I wanted to know what his friends thought of me. I met them the night before, some home from college for the summer.

"I do not. I can always catch them at the same bar stool at the same bar, if I do."

He didn't think I was funny. His cold eyes bore into mine, a sly grin spread across his face.

"They wanted to know, when I fucked you, did your vagina slant like your eyes."

If I had been older, had experienced more, and had varied relationships, I might have known better. But I was nineteen and inexperienced with verbal abuse, with misogyny. I thought he was mean and I did not like the smirk on his face. I glared at him until his ugly grin dissolved. The last remaining ember of supposed love I once had for him went out of my eyes and heart. Many years later I would see him again as a father to a five- year-old girl who he bullied and ridiculed in front of me, and to anyone else who wanted to listen. Oh, how I wished I had told that little girl she did not deserve to be spoken to that way. Then I should have knocked him out.

I would stay in that tumultuous relationship for two years. The dozen break ups were warm-ups. He was mean-spirited, and then repentant when he thought I would leave for good. I dated often at college, having been discovered by boys, but if there was a lull in my schedule, I called Patrick to come up for a visit, take me out to dinner. On breaks and holidays he was home, waiting.

The last year of our relationship, Patrick had a desire to go to college, to my college that I had transferred to in Minnesota. It was the last desperate attempt to hold on to our contentious relationship. We knew it was over months after he started school.

Whenever I heard stories of abused women or met someone who was, I could empathize with them. Everything is off kilter. A constant stunned state keeps you from thinking straight. It feels as though you are trapped underground, suffocating. You cannot find your way out. You lose a sense of normal. You don't know what love is; yet you know in your heart this cannot be it. You've an idea of what sort of relationship you want, seen enough examples of solid, healthy relationships to know what your aim is. You stumble out of the pitch, find your footing, your bearings. You tell yourself you will not fall into that abyss again.

⤚ᔆ

An awareness my Asian face and blackbrown hair were agreeable to men came to light, also during that spring break in Mazatlan with my Spanish class. Men in their twenties, a man more than twice my age, a businessman, who owned a good deal of the real estate, noticed me. This happened in the throes of body morphing, mood bending angst, and having gone unnoticed in our affluent school and community.

A girl who poured over Seventeen, Glamour, Cosmopolitan, People magazine, in search of a new and glamorous, *exotic* look.

I had heard the word *exotic* used to describe me, used when referring to Asian girls in general. But on that trip men used words, *beautiful, exotic*, to describe my face, my long dark hair. It was the businessman who sent over a pitcher of pina coladas to toast the beautiful young lady. He hoped she'd have a good time while in Mexico. Our heads swiveled this way and that way as we looked at one another uncertain who could be considered *beautiful*, a word usually reserved for women, not teenage girls. As the waiter placed the pitcher in front of me, our collective mouths dropped open. My mouth stayed slack the longest. The other girls sized me up, heads tilted from side to side, appraising, critiquing, trying to figure out what in the world made the man anoint me beautiful.

My (imperfect) feminist leanings came less from teachings learned in my Women's Studies classes. Instead, my education occurred in a bar. My best friend, Lisa, and I were headed towards a back booth at our regular watering hole when someone grabbed my butt, pinched it. Without thinking, I slapped the first face my hand could reach, one of four college boys crammed into a booth we had just passed.

"Hey, it wasn't me!" yelled the fellow whose face came in contact with my hand.

"I don't care which one of you it was. One of you is an asshole for pinching my ass and the rest of you are assholes for hanging out with the asshole." Lisa and I high fived each other, commenced to a booth, and once our beers came, we clinked our mugs in sister solidarity. *College boys can be such assholes.*

I shared with her the time my roommate in Texas got her butt bit by one of the frat boys, and then she dated him for months. We tried to articulate how these acts on our bodies and the rapes on campus that had occurred, were linked, though our language was just developing.

So I was not thrilled when all four of the original assholes had the nerve to show their faces at our booth. "Um, we'd like to apologize for pinching you. That wasn't cool and we're sorry.

"Um, yeah, sorry about that," they each said

"Yeah, it wasn't cool. Don't do it again," I said in a none-too-pleased voice.

"No, it won't happen again. Sorry."

Lisa and I agreed, however, that they were still assholes.

⁓

There were also opportunities to explore my sexuality with girls in college, but surprisingly, I did not want to cross that line. Boundaries were not my strength, but I knew in my heart I was not attracted to females, not sexually. I loved women, respected them deeply. There was nothing I loved more than being in the company of smart, funny, creative, self-confident girls and women. Because of this certainty of my own sexuality and my admiration for women, I was straightforward and honest, was not willing to disrespect, raise hopes of a relationship, when those moments arose. If only I could have applied that same integrity to other situations in my life....

⁓

I filled my time by gaining attention from boys and men. At a Minnesota college I was no longer invisible. I was noticed, sought out, and received too much attention. After graduating from college and moving to Minneapolis, young men were readily available at parties, in bars. Never one to dress provocatively, my Asian face seemed enough to ensure I did not have to go home alone.

What does a girl in her teens, in her twenties, do with this new-found knowledge but experiment and see where sexual play takes her? See what the power game of male, female dynamics is. See how far she can stretch, bend the game to her will. Maybe Patrick, my first long term relationship, was my litmus test, and since that did not go well, having tainted my perception, I abused that power. It became sport to serial date and collect men like rocks or stamps. In college I had a date with one fellow but I made sure Dave, whose crush on me made him amenable to do my bidding was positioned in a restaurant or party to take me away if I found the date less than exciting. Time after time he came to my rescue, drove me off in his black Trans Am. I could count on Rob and Tony to save me from a dull date too.

It was a thrill to acquire these notches on my "love" belt, though I convinced myself to not succumb to its pitfalls. They could fall in love with me, but I would not love them. Instead I chose to control boys and men, which offered nothing but emptiness.

I could not understand my actions, my attitude, for years. The sexual abuse by the retired judge that was never again mentioned left me angry, powerless, feeling unworthy. Being the new kid, the loneliness in high school, was made worse by lecherous stares from the advisor of the yearbook. The prospect of ending up alone in a room with him terrified me. I quit my position as co-editor my senior year. I would see this man decades later, and the same emotions would come over me. I left then, too. Bo's mom's beliefs, and his reluctance to disavow her stance confirmed what I suspected others believed. Perhaps he was testing the waters of what was acceptable, or not, within his family, by dating me. He would marry a woman who looked uncannily like his mother. My relationship with Patrick and his abusive attitude filled me with self doubt. Self-loathing. The professor, who hounded me, wrote letters over the summer, confronted me in a restaurant the following fall. *Why didn't you respond to any of my letters?* Who did not let up until I began to raise my voice at him, *You were my professor, I was your student, that's a boundary you should know better than to cross,* I practically yelled, with his colleague standing within earshot. He left abruptly.

Ever since I landed in Minnesota I had been pressed and flattened, ironed out any fibers of my being that might mark me as anything other than Minnesotan. I had so fully denied my Korean heritage that each time I saw my reflection I was puzzled; I could not connect with the face in the mirror. The features did not match who I believed myself to be. It was in direct conflict with the wider world that saw me as Asian and would not let me forget it.

When I filled out a form that asked for my ethnicity, I paused. Why must I check only Asian? But only one box could be checked. What about the Caucasian half of me that could not be detected on my face? What about the fact that I identified with my adoptive family in language, religion, and their Swedish heritage? Their ancestors were my ancestors. It was all I knew.

I would move my poised pen from the Caucasian box to the Asian box, and a momentary flash of thought, a wave of unformed curiosity would pass over me: I had lived in another land, spoken a different language, had been a part of another family. Why had I resisted, repressed, denied that existence, been so determined to bury and forget that life? But then, what good would it have done me to hold on to my Korean heritage? *How* could I have carried on the customs, the language? It was unrealistic to expect a child adopted from another country to maintain her culture when she did not see any evidence of it around her. But I had gone beyond just denying myself an understanding of things Korean. I had even refused to acknowledge that I was Korean.

During this transformation, this denial, I checked myself in any given situation to gain acceptance, followed the conventions, lived and worked among Caucasians, had only Caucasian friends. I was educated, well-mannered, one of them. No one could say I was fresh off the boat, spoke broken English. *Gook. Chink. Jap.*

Was the therapist on to something in suggesting I examine where I came from? Embrace my once-culture, my heritage? Reflect on my adoption? He encouraged me to consider that my denial of who and where I came from had everything to do with who I was to become.

Far in the back of my mind, thoughts of my biologic father were always near the surface. How he probably took advantage of my mother, like so many soldiers did, I believed, in Korea, Vietnam, the world over. I was conflicted. On the one hand, I loved men, knew more good males than bad in my life. But an unhealthy disregard towards them was becoming a problem I did not know how to handle.

～⌒

August 1991

It was your smile. My heart stopped and started again when you smiled at me. You make me feel alive. Harold said this to me again as he sat on my green armchair. It was awkward having him there, in my apartment. A familiar stranger, I often waited on him and his wife, who were considered regulars, coming in three to four times a month at the Greek restaurant. One night he pulled me aside to say my smile stopped his heart.

My smile. My fake smile. The one I adjusted and sometimes forced on my face to earn a living when many times it was the emotion I could least muster. He thought it was the real thing. That my smile reflected what was in my soul. How I was feeling. I could have won an award for my performance as a happy twenty-eight year old girl.

It was late summer, less than a month before the phone call, before everything changed. Harold had handed me his business card. If I ever needed anything, I could give him a call. He had written in his home phone number.

I could not fully trace back how he came to be in my apartment, sitting in my chair. Maybe it had something to do with my depression which was exacerbated by incessant partying and drinking. Was it triggered when I bumped into Ben on the street, and thought back on our relationship? How I hurt him? How callous I was towards him? What a fuck up I was?

I must have called Harold one night in a drunken state. That call led to several late nights of phone sex. The odd thing was, he never stated it was he. The stranger thing: I never asked whether it was.

I was in free fall.

Now there was a much older man in my apartment. It must have been boredom on my part, or a curiosity to see what happens when you invite an older man over, a man you've talked dirty to, that brought him here on a late afternoon.

Harold was in his mid sixties, average looking, with a bit of a belly, full head of hair though thinning a bit on top. There was nothing special about his appearance.

What I liked about him, ironically, was that he was a family man. It was clear he took good care of his wife's needs. The way he doted on her, leaning in and asking what she would like for dinner, making sure she took the first bite and that it met her approval. Perhaps that was what warmed me to him. Also, he beamed with pride when he talked about his children and grandchildren.

But that afternoon I saw something else in his eyes as he sat nervously looking at me and I at him. It was the same look when he talked about my smile and how it affected him. Throughout the rest of his dinner that night at the restaurant his eyes followed me, saw me anew. His expressions changed between intense eye contact to the old Harold, casual to my questions of another glass of wine? Dessert? Anything else I could get for them?

He was extremely kind, the type of man who gives you his full attention. Each time I waited on him and his wife we learned a bit more about the other. It seemed he could see through to my sad heart. His kind eyes said as much.

But the man in my living room was different from the one I had been waiting on for the past year. He looked at me with lust.

Harold arrived with a bottle of too sweet wine, baked goods and a book of poetry he never got around to showing me. He had brought, he said with nervous excitement, condoms.

I must have looked shocked. He apologized and said he didn't know what to expect, he wanted to be prepared, he wasn't sure....

There was no mention of the phone calls, the sex talks. Better to pretend as if we had not talked dirty to each other over the past weeks, like maybe it had been some random caller who had the wrong number and while he had me on the line he wanted to tell me how hard he wanted to fuck me. I was not one hundred percent sure it hadn't been a stranger.

I could not drink the wine, too sweet for my taste, as was the almond pastry. He was here in my apartment because he thought he was going to have sex with me. I invited him. Why did I invite him?

If he had approached me like he knew what he was doing, like he knew I was the one he wanted for all the right reasons, if he held me and caressed me and doted on me like I saw him do with his wife, then I could have been convinced of anything. But his lack of confidence actually annoyed me.

His lust had nothing to do with lovingly caressing or tenderly holding me. He would play with me for as long as he wanted. I could play with him too; even try to make him fall in love with me. But I was tired. Exhausted with that game. Nonetheless I tried to be a good host. He talked about his place in Florida, his extensive travels, his grandchildren. I mentioned my limited travels to Mexico and Belize, my love of scuba diving, my wanderlust, a desire to travel, to find where I belonged.

I began to get hot and clammy. I did not want to do this any more. "Harold, thanks for coming…"

"I should go?"

"Yah, I think so."

"Kate, you are a beautiful girl. I want you to know how alive I felt. Because of your smile, you stirred something in me that was dead. I can't deny I would like to make love to you—I know you don't want to. But I want you to know I care about you. If I can do anything…do you need money? I can help you, I can help you if you need money."

I was tempted. Mismanagement of money was a constant problem. I had accumulated some debt. Credit cards and a student loan I had ignored for months weighed on me. There were a number of parking tickets I had stuffed in a drawer and hoped would disappear. One of the reasons I moved was to get away from the incessant collection letters and telephone bombardments. (How naive I was: it did not stop the letters). I had been fired twice in the last year. The tips at the Greek restaurant were not enough to live on. I needed money. I needed to be taken care of. I wanted someone to take charge. To make my problems go away.

Before I moved to the apartment at the beginning of the summer, I mentioned to my sister I wanted to move back home for a while. I had not lived at home since the summer after my sophomore year of college. I just needed to regroup, get my act together. She warned my dad before I could ask. He was prepared with his reply. *No. You can do this. I believe you can take care of yourself. You're strong and capable. You can do it.* No amount of tears and begging changed his mind. I got angry. I hated him. He had not denied my siblings the opportunity to live at home. He offered to help consolidate my debt and co-sign a loan. I told him forget it, and hung up on him.

Here was my opportunity to free myself from my money woes. All I had to do was sleep with this man, a married man. Sleep with an old man. A grandpa. My money worries could disappear with a removal of my top and pants. I wondered how many times I'd have to gratify him before my debt would be nothing more than a bad memory.

I did not want to have sex with him. He was not handsome. He was old. Furthermore, I was not fond of being told what to do. I imagined, to participate in this age-old game, I would have to comply with his desires, be agreeable. Indulge him. Cook an occasional meal for him. I knew I could not take care of him in any capacity. I barely took care of myself.

I had been flabbergasted at my dad's refusal to offer me shelter. To save me from going the wrong way, save me from myself. Screw him. I would show him how sorry he would be for refusing to help me out in a time of need. But now I recalled my dad's words. How he believed I could take care of myself. How he knew I would find my way. Dad would not let me sink if he really thought I couldn't make it on my own. Right? Did he know something about me I had not yet figured out? He must have believed in me. He must believe I was strong. Capable. I knew the situation I was in now was not what he had in mind.

"Thanks, Harold, I'm okay."

"Let me help you, anytime."

"Thanks. I'll remember that."

"Let me help you."

"Thanks for coming, Harold."

"You'll let me know if you need anything."

"Yah. Yes, I will. Thanks."

After he left, I curled up in a ball on my bed. There was no limit to the disgust I felt with myself. There was no bottom to it.

9

November 1991

A chocolate cake, much like the one in the photograph from twenty-three years ago, rests on the dining room table, ready to be eaten. My American family is gathered at my parent's house to celebrate my twenty-ninth birthday with dinner and birthday cake. I have had chocolate cake with whipped cream layers or mocha layers—depending on my gastronomic hankerings, and always with chocolate frosting.

My hair, shoulder-length and lightened with reddish highlights is pulled back in a barrette. I either pay too much attention to my appearance, my clothes, looking overly made up or I put forth little effort. This day it is the latter. I wear a cheap off-white sweater, jeans and little makeup.

We are also gathered to make a video to send to my Korean family. Our family has expanded over the years. Peter is now married to Judy and they have an eighteen- month-old girl, Christina, with snowwhitehair. Tim is married to Geri and they also have an eighteen-month-old son, Derek, my godson. He, too, is fair-headed. AnnMarie and I are single, no children. Peter and Tim set up the camera while the rest of us clear cake plates from the dining room table.

I introduce myself first. "*Anyanghashimnika*, hello, peace be with you, Omma and Oppa." Except, of course, I butcher the long greeting. I don't know whether the O in Omma is a long O or short. I've mispronounced Oppa. I'm somewhat embarrassed to speak Korean because I cannot, even though I started taking private lessons. My tongue feels tied up with rope, Korean words no longer flow easily from my English speaking lips.

"I'm Kate. I used to be called Katie when I was younger, but now I'm Kate, it just sounds mature. Today's my birthday. I just turned twenty-nine." I am a blathering idiot. Clearly I have not rehearsed what I'm going to say, so typical of me to wing it.

"I'm looking forward to seeing all of you someday, soon. Um, please call me Anny. Yeah. Anny. I would like it if you call me Anny. Okay. I know Oppa and I have talked about seeing each other some time in the near future. I hope we do. Bye."

Peter introduces himself, his wife, Judy, and Christina. Peter is the big brother, the loyal and dependable one. He is the optimist, always cheerful, hard working. Tim and Geri hold Derek, say a greeting and express their enthusiasm over our new family.

Mom and dad take turns exclaiming how wonderful it is that Omma, Oppa, his wife, and three daughters will be part of our family. We are all thrilled and feel incredibly blessed.

It is AnnMarie's turn. "Hi, I'm AnnMarie, I just want to say how wonderful it is that Oppa has found Kate, found all of us. We're so excited to get to know our Korean family. I always wanted a sister, I begged mom and dad for one and then they adopted Kate. I finally got a big sister. I hope to meet you some day. Bye."

I am not sure if I heard her correctly. Did she say she had wanted a sister and that's why my parents adopted me? For twenty-three years I never got a straight answer as to why I was adopted. *We wanted to adopt an older child who needed a home. We felt we could do that for a child.* But where was the starting point of the adoption thread when they already had three children on a pastor's salary?

Can this really be the reason? I was adopted because AnnMarie wanted a sister? This explained so much. Namely, whatever AnnMarie wanted, AnnMarie received, even a sister plucked away from her family on the other side of the world. I had been her toy, her plaything, adopted to entertain and amuse her, to keep her from feeling lonely. It is unsettling to know the truth, and to find out this way. I cannot stop staring at her as my mind roils and all sorts of feelings come to the surface.

But I do what I have learned to do: I push the emotions down. Stifle the questions rising up in my throat. Resist the urge to stop everything, demand answers. Instead, I will continue to make everyone around me laugh and lighten spirits.

For some reason, there is polka music playing on the stereo. "I've never learned how to polka," I say instead. Geri says she will teach me. Tim gets out the video camera and Geri and I dance around the kitchen, through the large living room, dining room and around, again and again. I whoop it up, call out to Derek and Christina to join in on the action. The children giggle joyfully at being included in the merriment and silliness with their mom and aunt. Now this feels like a party.

～6～

In January, I move in with my sister and her roommate to save money for the next five months before I leave. They live on the upper two levels of a large old house that was converted into an apartment. The owners live on the main floor. The living room is now my bedroom, which consists of my futon that can be rolled up during the day and stowed away for the rare occasion the room is used for its original purpose. My contribution to the household is my tear stained armchair that they will use upstairs in the TV nook. My suitcases overflowing with clothes are my only other belongings. The kitchen table and two chairs and side table are stored in my parent's basement. I have prided myself on living with little. It is all the easier to pick up and move on when you have few possessions.

It is a good arrangement, a win-win for all of us until her roommate wants me to pay more of the monthly rent than we originally agreed on. This leads to fights between my sister and me about breaking verbal contracts and her unwillingness to stand up for me. She feels she is put in an awkward position; she wants me to buck up and go along with the rent hike.

Mom gets involved. She offers to pay the difference in the rent increase. She knows I am saving every penny for my trip.

My mom's attention directed on me is strange. Stranger still is how uncomfortable I feel when she comes to my aid. I am not used to her siding with me *and* giving me money. Further, I'm still adjusting to my parent's magnanimous gift of paying for my round trip airfare to Korea.

On one of the last nights before my departure, my mom calls me into her bedroom. She sets down her heavy wooden jewelry box between us on her bed, and withdraws a black velvet satchel. I know what is inside. It is a large oval shaped jade ring that Grandmother gave her, and her other daughter-in-laws from a trip she took to Japan.

Often when I was young I snuck into her room and tried on the ring. I had wanted it from the first moment I saw it. To my young eyes the moss green jade was as large as an egg, even more so on my bony finger. With its thin gold band and delicately etched base encircling the stone, it was both feminine and solid. A number of times I had asked her if I could have it. She always said no. *She might wear it some day.* Now, she wants me to have it.

"I never wore this," she says, holding it in her palm.

"I've always loved it."

She gestures for me to take it. "I know you have. It suits you, as if it was made for your hand."

We hug each other, and as I thank her, she gives me an extra squeeze of love.

⸺ഗ⸺

The corner of my mouth has broken out in a cold sore. It's red and raw and it hurts. I leave for Korea in a week and suddenly I am afraid to go. *What if my family doesn't like me?* My greatest fear is they might say or silently conclude that it was no big loss to give me away after all. Since I have not done much with my life. Since my college education has been wasted. Omma was upset to learn I waitress for a living, and it didn't help when Dr. Kim, my Korean language teacher, confirmed that in Korea, to work in a restaurant is considered a lowly position.

I am not the success story I should be. The story where the Korean daughter is given away at six goes off to the richest country in the world and vows to make something of herself. She is scary smart, educated at one of the top colleges in the nation, and works for one of the fortune five hundred companies until she marries a proper man, which means he makes a lot of money. They have loads of children, who will be wildly successful. She makes the best kimchi, keeps a clean and orderly house. She is an upstanding member of society, involved in the community and assorted charities. She gives of her time unselfishly, devotedly to others, always to others. Not one bit of that story is mine.

I wonder if my Korean family and I can write letters instead. Talk on the telephone every so often. I begin to obsess and lose sleep over what I call my hamster wheel thoughts. My thoughts run on a wheel that goes around and around.

I have not done a thing with my life. I worry Omma will not think I am a good daughter. Here was my second chance at life and it looks like I squandered it. I don't know what to do with myself. I don't know how to speak Korean. I am American. There is nothing Korean about me. What does it mean to be Korean? What does it mean to have been Korean once and are no longer? Will the Korean part come out while I'm in Korea? Like syrup from a maple tree, if you know when and where to tap it, syrup will flow. If somehow my brain is tapped, metaphorically speaking, will the Korean part of me spill out into the proverbial syrup bucket?

I cannot go to Korea. I don't want to face the mother who gave me away with high expectations that I would do something important, or at the very least I would be good—whatever that meant. There is nothing I have accomplished on that success list. I do not want to see the disappointment on Omma's face. I can stay home and see disappointment by looking in the mirror.

But I cannot cancel this trip. Omma, Oppa and his family, and who knows who else in Korea, are expecting me. I must go back to my birth country, a country where I am ignorant of the culture, the language, and the people. That is a whole lot of ignorance. All the years of becoming a Minnesotan, a good Swedish girl in denial of her Korean ethnicity has taken its toll. I spent twenty-three years disavowing, discarding, disowning my Korean identity. I have contributed to my own ethnic cleansing.

⸎

May 7, 1992

On the flight to Los Angeles, I ponder some information that dad gave me to read on my last visit with him and mom. I am not sure what to make of it. It was a research paper about the Korean War between North and South Korea. The war started in 1950, with the United States defending South Korea and China, North Korea. This report was focused more on Korean women's lives during the war. How the hardships of survival drove many women into prostitution at nearby U.S. army bases. How prostitution was encouraged by the Korean government, even touted as patriotic. As a result, thousands of Amerasians, half American half Korean babies were born, as well as many Eurasians, children of European soldiers. The Korean people, a homogenous group living in the land known as the "hermit kingdom," did not accept these mixed children. Half black half- Korean, or half-Korean half Caucasian children were shunned by society, along with their mothers. They were a source of shame to the pure lineage of this ancient ethnic people. The Korean government allowed these Amerasian children, and full-blooded Korean children to be adopted in the United States and Europe. At first it was a trickle, of which I was one of the first adoptees to Minnesota. By the early nineteen nineties, there would be well over one hundred thousand Korean children adopted in the United States.

I grew up seeing only negative images of Asian girls, women on television. In the rare occasion an Asian girl or woman appeared on the screen, she was reduced to an unidentifiable Asian status; rarely was her ethnicity differentiated. Except for the TV show MASH. It was understood they were Koreans only because the show took place in Korea during the Korean War. But on the show Koreans were in the background, seen as less than human, living in squalor, silently accepting their miserable lot in life. I was humiliated at the limited portrayal of Koreans and their culture, which reinforced my disconnection.

On the big screen, too, one size fits all Asian girls and women were portrayed negatively: as prostitutes who were at the mercy of a white man, as asexual grinds working themselves to death, as asexual nerds, living to solve a complex math equation, or as a caricature, in floppy pigtails and little girl's clothing, laughing behind their hands, speaking broken English, *I solly, hee hee*. The Asian woman never got to be beautiful or have a boyfriend. If she was paired with a male, usually in commercials, he was almost always black. Never was she with an Asian male. If she was with a white man, he was her savior. Not his equal. She was never seen as successful. Or accomplished. Never recognized as *wholly complex*.

I would scour magazines, watch TV, or movies, holding my breath, waiting to see a face similar to mine represented out there in a positive way. I did not see Asian women or girls (not to mention Asian men) making ingenuous, innovative, important contributions. They did not exist. The only Asian woman with any name recognition was Connie Chung, a CBS anchorwoman. Even though we looked nothing alike, people seemed to think we did. She was also much older than me; I could not identify with her. Furthermore, she was Chinese.

The report that dad gave me seemed to confirm what I believed, that many of the servicemen took advantage of hapless Korean women who were doing whatever they had to for survival. That the Korean government encouraged this is reprehensible.

As I got older, I had little tolerance for a man in uniform because my biologic father was probably one of these men. I believed my mother was probably at the mercy of my father, an American serviceman who used her, had his fun with her. When she became pregnant with me, he probably abandoned her. Being half Caucasian and half Korean I was probably rejected by the Korean culture. My mother probably could not take care of me because I was a stigma, a shame.

My dad said he did not want me to get my hopes up, that I should go to Korea with eyes wide open. That the same plight that fell on so many Korean women might be Omma's story too. I knew his intentions were good, but I feel uneasy, conflicted. Am I really better off armed with this information?

Part Two
KOREA

I am not the same
having seen the moon shine
on the other side of the world.

MARY ANNE RADMACHER

10

May 1992

The airplane lands at Kimpo Airport. It is nearly midnight. *I arrived in Minnesota at midnight.* This full circle moment is not lost on me. Twenty-three years ago I was at this same airport, except the airplane was facing the other way, towards the red, white and blue of amber waves of grain and purple mountains.

I am not ready. I sit and gather myself. I'm hot, clammy. My insides rev like a Nascar at the starting line, my heart is beating too fast, ready to burst. Nausea. Panic. Excitement. I want to jump out of my seat, but I am glued to it, paralyzed.

And again, just like all those years ago, I have no idea what awaits me on the other side.

Kyung, a Korean American woman, who lives in Los Angeles with her husband and two teenage sons also remains seated. She goes back to Korea once a year to visit her family. She and I shared our stories during the fifteen hour flight. She is surprised and saddened, yet hopeful, for my journey.

She takes my hand and holds it tight. She understands the intensity of this moment, has tears in her eyes. "God bless you, Kate. I hope the very best for you on your journey." She cannot imagine what it must be like coming back to this land and reconnecting with people who were once my family. "I will pray for you and I will never forget you. Thank you for sharing your story with me. I am honored." She gives me a hug, a hug filled with happiness for a young woman about to meet her family.

Her sincerity and genuine interest made it easy to open up to her. Kyung held my hand and even cried with me at various points of my telling. I most likely will never see her again, but I will not forget her either. Her hug is strong and loving. Maybe I cling to her a bit longer than she expected. I am not quite ready to go at this alone. Her arms around me give me strength. She holds me until I am ready. She is wise, understanding; I imagine she is a good mother, a good friend.

She gives one more wave good-bye before disappearing into the waiting embrace of her family.

Twenty-three years ago, I left from this airport with very little. Omma had packed my hanbok and a black silk purse in a brown paper bag. I wore the simple red dress and red tennis shoes. Pearl earrings, a yellow plastic purse with a note tucked inside for my adoptive family.

This time, I am dressed in loose wide-legged black slacks and a cream colored blouse. My disheveled shoulder length hair pulled back in a barrette. I have two suitcases, and a carry-on, all packed to maximum capacity. So much that I'm concerned they might burst open mid flight. I had to apply all my weight and knee pressure along the zipper to get it closed. In my extra large suitcase, I've packed summer and some cold weather clothes for the undetermined length of my stay. The mid-size suitcase holds gifts for my family. In the carry-on case I have a Sony CD player Oppa requested, an English-Korean dictionary, some books, and a journal.

I was proud the day I received the three-piece luggage set as a high school graduation gift from my parents. This was no ordinary gift I told myself, it had serious symbolic implications: it represented traveling to unknown parts, to uncharted territories as far as my desires, curiosity could take me. The luggage meant onto other places (warmer climes, I hoped), exploration, discovery of new lands, and ultimately to discovery of myself. I saw all that in my cheap vinyl three piece maroon Arrival luggage.

I lugged it to college in Texas, and then back to Minnesota. It had been to California where I visited Patrick. I cringe remembering how I had taken the large suitcase on wheels to Mexico and Belize for two weeks with Ben. How I had insisted on packing it with high-end clothes from working in Dayton's Oval Room. How inappropriate the clothes were on the tiny backpacking island of Caye Caulker, how it almost broke the boat driver's back as he attempted to lift the weight of deeply discounted designer clothing onto the dock.

I like to think I am more practical now. That my clothes and all the accoutrements I've carted to this country will be needed, be of use.

—6

The last of my over-packed suitcases slides down the conveyor belt and onto a metal carousel. It's an unwieldy load I heft onto a cart. As I walk around to the back of the cart to steer it, the wide pant leg that almost grazes the floor catches on my right shoe. I trip. There's a collective gasp among the passengers who witness my clumsiness. *Aigoo! Aigoo,* I hear around me. Tongues clicking. Concerned looks. People start to move towards me. "No problem. I'm fine," I say, jumping up. They smile in relief. Embarrassed, I push my unhip vinyl luggage towards customs. Some continue to glance over to make sure I'm truly okay or maybe they think, *what a klutz.* My face feels hot, my cheeks, flushed. This is far from the smooth entrance I imagined.

I follow other travelers as they seem to know where to go. It is a long line through customs where my blue passport is looked at briefly, stamped, and I am sent on my way. There are frosted glass double doors to get through, the last barrier before I meet my family. My heaping cart begins to turn left on its own accord, away from the doors. Steering the free-wheeling cart is a welcome distraction from the reoccurring obsessive questions that rush forth again. What if my family doesn't like me? What if we have absolutely nothing in common? What if they reject me? My heart is pounding. I am certain it is going to jump out of my chest cavity and make its way back on the airplane.

The double doors open automatically. A rush of voices rises up. A sea of dark heads, Korean faces stand waiting. Hundreds of Korean eyes are glued to the doors. A momentary silence, collective breaths held: *will this person be ours?*

I am taken by surprise at the number of Korean people amassed before me. I have never been in any setting where the landscape has been filled entirely with Koreans. How will I find Oppa and Omma? I should have planned ahead by letting them know what I would be wearing.

The throng of greeters resume their talk once they realize I am not who they wait for. But I notice a movement somewhere in the middle of the room. It is the slightest disturbance, a rustling, like how prairie grass ripples when someone walks through the tall stalks. This someone is a little woman with one arm out plowing her way through the blockade of people. They try to get out of her way or are forcefully shoved aside by this diminutive person. She rushes to the rope the demarcation that divides greeters and the newly arrived.

She jumps up and down, waves, shouts, "Anny! Anny!" She is oblivious of the rope; anyway, it will not be able to hold her back. Her eyes lock on mine. Her face, layered with wild emotions, of joy, of yearning. "Anny! Anny! Annyyyy!"

I cannot take my eyes off of her. This is my mother. This is my Omma. I cannot breathe. I cannot think. I feel faint and anxious all at once. I imagine my expression is similar to that of a deer caught in the headlights: stunned, unable to move.

She grabs my arm with such force, such strength, I yelp. She latches onto my arm and pulls at me, runs me down the length of the rope barrier, a metaphorical DMZ, 38th parallel, the only barrier keeping us apart, until we are at the end of it. All the while she calls out my name. She yanks me towards her, "Anny!" In the seconds before Omma clutches me to her, her eyes bore into mine; mine into hers. We take in as much as we can of each other before she throws herself at me and wails into my neck.

A keening wail of stifled longing, wild and wounded. Hers. Mine. Weeping, so much weeping. Surely our sorrowful tears will flood the airport. Omma clings to me. I hold onto her with all my might. "Omm.... Omma...." I can barely speak. The words come out in a choked whisper.

"Anny...Anny...."

"Omma...Omma...."

Omma and I are cried out, but we continue to hold each other. "Anny... Anny...." She murmurs my name over and over, almost as a lamentation. Her hold on me has loosened, but by no means is she going to let go. I feel a presence to my right, and as I turn my red and teary eyes, I latch onto the kindest, warmest ones. This is my big brother.

"Anny, *dongsaeng*," Oppa says, in a somber voice. He chokes as he says little sister. We grab each other. Our sobs erupt from a locked place, of grief, sorrow, heartache.

We hold each other in this awkward way, Omma, sandwiched in between Oppa and me. We continue to cry at our loss, and our reunion. Oppa's daughters and wife are there on the periphery, but no one interrupts us. They wait patiently for us to cross a two decade chasm.

The three of us pull apart just enough to include Oppa's family. His wife, my sister-in-law, *eonni*, hands me a yellow handkerchief with a knowing look. I thank her for her thoughtfulness as I pat my wet face and blow my nose. She gives me a quick hug without words and pushes her oldest daughter, Ah Young, towards me in lieu of a verbal greeting. My niece tries out her stilted self-conscious English, "Welcome, Komo. I am Ah Young."

"Hello, Ah Young. I'm so happy to meet you," I say, giving her a hug. I turn to shy Ah Rim, give her a big hug and repeat the same sentiment. Ah Hee holds a large bouquet of fragrant tiger lilies in front of her face like a shield. I try to catch a glimpse of her. In between the curls of white and pink petals I glimpse the face of a mischievous fun-loving girl. She smiles, exposing crooked teeth. But she is too shy to give me the flowers. She uses them instead as a screen to hide behind. Ah Hee begins to say something in English, but she doesn't trust herself. She succumbs to rapid fast Korean. Whatever she said has the rest of the family laughing. I give her an extra long hug, grateful to her for breaking the tension.

11

Oppa's apartment is in a newer development. The term apartment means something different in Korea. It is similar to condominiums in that they are owned by the dweller, but these apartments are built on a large scale like Western apartments. His home is up three short flights of stairs. There are three bedrooms the largest is Oppa's and eonni's. One entire wall is a built-in closet for their bedding and clothes. The medium size room is Ah Rim's and Ah Hee's. Ah Young has the smallest. But she has given up her room to me. She stays in a small room Oppa has in the basement of the building.

Oppa has bought a Western style green bed set, matching dresser, mirror, chair and armoire for me. I wish he hadn't done this. I wanted to live the Korean experience by sleeping on the floor like the rest of my family.

In the living room, a Western style dark green leather couch and armchair faces a large TV that remains on at all hours. Sliding glass doors open to a balcony that extends to Oppa and eonni's room. Out here is where eonni has her washer and a clothesline.

Eonni sets a table in the kitchen for our meals. Each morning she has an entire breakfast ready by the time I wake up. We usually eat some sort of fish soup, or grilled fish with *pan chan*, side dishes of vegetables along with white rice. It will take some adjusting to eat like this.

The *ondol* floor throughout the apartment is heated by heating coils, which was invented in 1000 B.C. Back in earlier times it was heated from underneath, below ground, by a wood stove. The stove warmed the entire upper floor where the family ate and slept. The floor is now heated with electricity. It is from the warmed floor I sit and begin to get to know my family.

Omma has a hardy laugh. Her eyes light up behind her large gold-rimmed glasses when she laughs or smiles. She walks with a straight back (apparently I did not get this trait from her, I slouch). She is similar to other Korean women in height: short, at about five feet tall. Omma tucks her withered hand into the waistband of her pants or skirt. Her voice is deep and hoarse, due to smoking cigarettes a good part of her life. She constantly tells me to, *eat some. You eat? Eat some. Eat some more.* She does not think I eat enough. I have never been accused of this in my life!

Oppa is staying home from his company my first week. His assistant will run his printing company. He takes me to see his company, to meet his employees. Afterwards we walk around the business district of Seoul. People he knows stop to greet us; they think Oppa and I are the same age. He does look more my age than thirty-nine. His face, handsome, smooth like freshly scooped vanilla ice cream, his eyes, kind and intelligent. He has full lips, like Omma, which I envy. Oppa dresses in upscale suits, probably hand tailored, of pale green, grey green. While his smiles are rare, when he does, the sun dims. I will do anything to see him grin. His laughter comes from a depth, untapped. My heart flutters at the sound of his laughter.

At fifteen, Ah Young is the boldest of my three nieces. She's anxious to learn English and practices with me as often as possible, carries her Korean/English dictionary with her. Because they all want to try out their English, no one wants to speak Korean to me. Which is going to make it difficult for me to learn the language.

Oppa says Ah Rim is a good artist and very intelligent; she's one of the top students in her class. She looks like Oppa. We smile at each other; she blushes and turns away with a small smile.

Eleven-year-old Ah Hee, a bit of a tomboy with scrappy knees and mussed up hair, watches me from across the room, but willingly accompanies the adults on evening walks.

On one of the first days, as Ah Hee and I walk towards the door on an errand, Omma watches us. "Anny. You, Ah Hee, walk same-same." She stands up and mimics our gangly loose limb walk. She repeats her remark to Ah Hee in Korean. Ah Hee grins and blushes. She looks at me; I smile and put my arm around her.

Ah Hee and I fall into an easy routine of going to the local mom and pop stand down the street. It is the Korean version of a small Seven Eleven or Super America, without the gas pumps. These stores are on every corner making it handy for those last minute needs. There is a randomness in both location and structure, of hodgepodge boards, nails and green plastic roofs that make me think: minimal regulations and license required. Produce is sold outside the small building under green plastic awnings. Inside there are no sheetrock walls or organized shelving units, only what seems to be arbitrary wooden shelves and crates displaying an assortment of merchandise. Ah Hee and I load up on fruit and chocolates. She and I like Hershey's Kisses. We get dried fish, *ojinga,* that Oppa and Omma like, and alcoholic beverages, Soju for Oppa, and beer for me. We have something for everyone.

I see some of the trappings of Seoul, or at least the popular tourist destinations in this city of 10 million. Oppa and Omma are eager to show me the sights and I oblige, even though I am not your average tourist seeking beauty in this *land of the morning calm* peninsula. Enriching myself with its ancient culture takes a backseat now that I am reunited with my family. But this is my family's country and city and I hope to glean some understanding of their culture from these excursions.

We take a boat ride on the Han River. From this vantage point I am able to take in the sprawl that is Seoul, horizontally and vertically.

Along the river, incredibly tall white buildings, mostly apartments, cram the landscape, with constant construction taking up every inch of land. Because land is finite, many of the buildings are built upward where sky is the limit.

We visit King Sejong's palace and grounds. He was the ruler during the Choson Dynasty, during The Golden Age. He is referred to as "The Great," and it seems for good reason. He brought about *han'gul*, the Korean language. He had the political foresight to institute this phonetic writing system and language. He wanted a language that was not dependent on the complicated Chinese writing, an important political achievement.

Oppa takes me to Olympic Park, the pride of most Seoulites and Koreans. I remember the 1988 Olympics. I watched with fascination the opening and closing ceremonies and listened to the commentaries about Korea where the world witnessed Korea's debut. It was the Korean people's moment to say to the world: We have arrived. The Chinese and Japanese might have raped and pillaged our people and land, but they cannot invade our souls. Nor can the Korean War (technically still at war) that divides the two countries into north and south. We are a hard-working, well-educated, prosperous country with the exportation of steel. We have risen from our ashes of oppression and invasion; mark us on your maps, we will show you what we are made of.

My heart had swelled with pride, surprisingly, as NBC's cameras panned the beautiful country, and captured the warmth and mirth of the Korean people. They highlighted Korean artistry from pottery to calligraphy, the high literacy rate, and touted their economic growth through exportation of steel and cars.

I also watched the Olympics with the childish fantasies (at twenty six) of catching a glimpse of my mother. I imagined perhaps she'd be an honorary representative for Korea: *Ladies and gentlemen, this woman is the face of Korea. She gave away her daughter when her girl was six years old.* The camera pans a close-up of my mother, while the announcer says, *This is Anny's mother. Anny, if you're out there, contact your mother.*

NBC's Today Show host, Bryant Gumble, informed viewers that Koreans are considered the Irish of the East. That got me excited because I'd believed I was part Irish. In my mother's one letter sent to my parents she had signed her last name Kang, but the handwriting looked like Kane. Somehow I got the notion Kane was Irish. I fabricated a scenario of what this implied. I believed my father was Irish or maybe Scottish and that she had taken his last name during their time together.

Bryant Gumble went on to say Koreans, generally speaking, are a hot-tempered bunch, having presumably the same heated temperament as the Irish. I remembered Ben giving me a side-ways look and mumbling, *I tremble in fear, a whole country of them like you.* I could not have been prouder.

‿ below

Eonni does not say much. Each morning before I wake she has already done her hair and make-up. She looks glamorous, has expensive tastes. She gives me a smile when we catch each other's eyes. She cannot speak English. We resort to pantomiming or Omma steps in to help translate.

She thinks my clothes are shabby. From the start she was dismayed by my sleepwear, an over-sized, threadbare turquoise t-shirt with holes under the armpits. She cannot believe I wear this to bed. I was unable to explain to her that this is precisely why it's the perfect sleepwear. She continues to eye it. I think she's secretly plotting to get rid of it.

Eonni's sister and husband want to take me shopping. I have no idea about this until we are at Lotte Department store. It is what the

Mall of America is to Minnesota, but this place has been around much longer than the MOA. It is enormous, with a four star hotel, bowling alleys, an ice rink, amusement rides and couture boutiques. Uniquely it has a huge market in the basement where Seoulites can get Western products such as the metal mesh coffee filter and American coffee Oppa purchased for me once he realized I like coffee and needed it in order to be a nice person.

My family is on a mission here, to buy me things. Eonni wants to get me a proper pair of pajamas since she cannot get the holey T-shirt out of her mind. We walk up and down aisles and she and her sister stop every few feet, ask if I like the thing. I keep saying *anni*, no. I have no idea we will not leave until I say *ne*, yes. They stop at a full-length sheepskin leather coat. I am not remotely interested; it looks expensive, and because it's about ninety degrees out. The sisters talk nonstop while scrutinizing the coat. I can tell eonni has a discerning eye, can see the true value and craftsmanship of things. She reminds me of the clientele who shopped at The Oval Room, the haute couture section of Minneapolis's beloved department store.

They want me to have that coat. "Anni, anni. No, no. No thanks," I say, practically running away as they pull the coat off the mannequin.

We keep walking up and down aisles. At some point eonni's sister sizes up my purse. I bought the purse before coming to Korea. It suited my taste: black leather with brushed silver buckles (very uptown) and a long strap so I could wear it over my shoulder and across my torso. I think they both find it cheap and common. I also brought a brown leather purse but I know it does not pass eonni's high standards. Unbeknownst to me, the sisters have made up their minds. I am to have a new purse.

We walk into a boutique. I no longer desire the boutique or designer-made clothes and accessories like I once did when I modeled, while experimenting with becoming a yuppie. During that time

I worked as a sales consultant at the couture and high-end designer clothing store, Dayton's Oval Room, in downtown Minneapolis. I was a slave to the deep, deep discount rack, but it was still designer clothing, I told myself. Every penny I made went back into the Dayton's coffer. Once I quit, I decided I would no longer be ruled by fashion.

Eonni holds up different handbags with matching wallets and I steadily shake my head, no. I think I hesitated at some point over one, because the next thing I know, eonni has taken my cheap purse and replaced it with an Italian black and brown leather purse and matching wallet. I am dismayed. "No, no, *anni, anni.* Thanks but no thanks." I say, vehemently shaking my head, with my hand out in a halt, stop position. "No. No, thank you." That purse is probably worth more than I made in a month. I cannot bear the thought of my extended family spending such an exorbitant amount.

By late afternoon, I am back at Oppa's place with a new striped silk bathrobe (to cover up the offensive T-shirt) and the Italian leather purse and wallet.

12

The garlic! mounds and mounds of garlic. Never in my life have I seen so much of it. In every market, wherever there is produce, strands of garlic ropes stacked waist high can be found. It is something to behold, an art form to this foreigner's eyes. In Minnesota only individual bulbs are found at the grocery store.

You smell it first, fish, all sorts of bizarre fish. Long thin silver fish, smaller round fish, bright orange lumpy things, which I'm not certain are considered fish. There's octopus, and so much more. They swim about in big plastic or metal bins innocent of the fate that awaits them. Water is everywhere as fishmongers clean and cut up into bite size pieces whatever you choose to eat.

At the market, you have to have your wits about you to navigate among the vendors who are busily making a living. They have no time to tread carefully around a foreigner who sort of looks like one of their own countrymen, but has no clue how much she is impeding their work. People jostle me from all directions. I'm big on personal space, but no one seems to notice my scowl from being bumped into, pushed and generally shoved around.

There is a smell about the place that is offensive to this American who has become sensitive to any sort of unpleasant scents. Americans do not permit noxious fumes to waft through the air! It's just not done. Here, it's a daily assault, a combination of fish, seawater, garlic, car and bus exhaust, city sewers and a host of other unidentifiable odors.

Eonni buys a watermelon and all sorts of green vegetables I cannot name. We sit at one of the fish stands for a bite of the fresh fish of the day. You cannot get fresher fish than this! I try a bite of every fish on the table, but it is the kochujang dipping sauce, of red pepper paste with cider vinegar, sugar, salt, and sesame oil that gets my attention. I want to drink the stuff, but I think I might come off looking like a tourist. Instead I slather a good amount on my lettuce with a small amount of fish. I am beginning to acquire a love for the food.

It is the bright orange pieces of fish I like best. Omma notices. "Anny, you young time, you like so much. Eat too much this."

"Oh, I remember this taste, I do!" I say, surprised. My sense memory recalls this flavor. I'm stunned at how strong this flavor memory is. "It's so good." I want more. Omma is thrilled. She orders another serving of the mung gi just for me. I am loath to share, but I do.

We are once again walking through the market when another familiar scent hits my nostrils. I cannot identify it. *What is it?* We weave through stalls, winding our way out of Karak Market when I'm struck with the memory of this smell that wafts and dominates the air. "What, what you smell?" Omma asks. She looks around trying to locate the scent. I have my nose in the air sniffing, sniffing as I walk. Steam is coming from a large barrel. My nose tells me this is what I smell. Except now it is not a pleasant odor. I cannot say it was a in the first place, but my initial excitement was at recalling it from my childhood.

"This is it, I remember this smell as a little girl!" I shout. "What is it?" An old woman wearing a white hat that resembles a beekeeper's hat stands by the barrel. She has gloves on and a large ladle in her hand.

"Ah, Anny, baby time you like so much!" Omma says, jumping up and down at the memory.

"What is it?" I ask again, as the ajimma opens the lid. An explosion of steam billows out making it difficult to see what's inside.

"How you say in English?" Omma says. She cannot recall at first. "Ah, Anny, silkworms, silkworms!" Omma says, as she pays the ajimma a few coins for…silkworms.

My stomach begins to roil. In a white cone-shaped cup is a heap of cooked brown silkworms, boiled to perfection, awaiting eager eaters to consume them.

"Uh…really…silkworms. I ate these?"

"You like so much. Good for you too. Make you strong." Omma thrusts the cup into my hand. She looks up at me and laughs. "You maybe no like anymore." I nod my head in agreement. I tell myself to try it, but I cannot work up the nerve.

⁓

I walk the streets of Seoul and no one notices me. No one does a double take. No one looks at me once, twice, to discern what ethnicity has just passed by. I blend in. I am the similar face that in-mass shuffles onto the subway or the bus or walks down the bustling streets of Seoul. To Seoulites I am another Korean going about my business of living in this incredibly alive productive city.

Seoulites have a no nonsense attitude about them, which may be the common denominator of those living in big cities. They do not seem to mettle in other people's actions or behaviors. Once in a while, if I say something in English and a person overhears me on a bus or subway, they glance at me with mild interest. Usually they are not curious enough to strike up a conversation.

Only the ajimmas seem to stop and give me a long stare, if I speak. *Ajimma*, aunt, is the name used to refer to women out in public who are older, middle class. It is the ubiquitous term for all women outside of your family. *Ajashi* is uncle. I was told this comes from the belief that Koreans, who are a homogenous people, believe they are all related; everyone has a 'family' name connecting them. The ajimmas look at me with surprise, confusion. They seem to be thinking, *the facial features cannot be trusted to tell the whole story. She is not one of us. She speaks with a strange tongue.*

I notice something. It is my shoulders. They are no longer bunched up grazing my ears. Rather, my shoulders are relaxed and stress-free. Most of my life I have been on guard, alert to my surroundings, aware that people saw me as different. You are watchful of how others perceive you. You adjust accordingly. You do what you can to put them at ease. You must. You are the outsider.

But here, oh, blessed land of my facial features and dark hair, you do not question or doubt my presence. You do not readily mark me foreign or *other*. Instead you let me pass as one of your own, as part of the majority. You render my body unclenched.

Oh, how sweet to exhale.

_6

It is shocking, the poverty that overflows and lives beside prosperity and affluence, a startling contrast, out in the open, not hidden under bridges and dense shrubbery like in Minneapolis. Here, the homeless are squeezed in and around every block alongside shiny new construction. Endless construction on limited land.

Just outside Oppa's big picture window in the living room is a view of a shabby commune, a hodgepodge of small shacks contained by a six foot cement-like wall. It's remarkable what people use for shelter. There is cardboard, plastic tarps, plywood, scrap lumber, metal, all haphazardly thrown together or perhaps as it is acquired. What is more unsettling is how many people constantly come out of the dozen or so ramshackle structures. Where is their bathroom? Mangy flea-infested dogs tied up just outside the make shift doors look hungry.

Oppa says they have to be out by this fall. The city needs the land for more housing, for real housing. "Where will they go?" I ask him, standing at the window, looking out at the shacks. He doesn't know. They will probably set up homes in another undeveloped area until that too becomes a lucrative development.

Invasion, war and poverty are a part of the history and heritage of Korea and its people. It is evident among the elderly, deeply ingrained on their faces. They have lived harsh and difficult lives. Lines etched on their faces mark the burdens and sorrows they have suffered. Was there happiness? A moment to sit and enjoy the sunset? A time for reflection? To ponder if this is what they wanted out of their life? Is this it? Survival leaves little room for frivolity.

The young epitomize modern Korea. How they contrast against the old. The prosperous against the poor, the ten million people over-crowding Seoul, against the diminishing life of the country. The tra-ditions and customs: of speech, of dress, are becoming second rate compared with the onslaught, the bombardment of western con-sumption of goods and influences. Capitalism, not even three hun-dred years old compared with the thousands of years Koreans have lived with Kings and courts. Now it seems Korea is in a death-lock of capitalistic overkill.

Nowhere do you notice this more than with the young. The young with their Western hair cuts, American music, brands and labels pol-luting their bodies and minds. Will it be McDonald's tonight? KFC? Pizza Hut? Come dressed in your best Nike's T-shirt and tennis shoes.

Get out of the rice fields, off the farms, you bumpkins, live the good life in the city of lights and action all night long. There is no life for you in the rural countryside, it's too difficult to make a living. Seoul is where it is at.

As the old die off, so, presumably, will much of the backbone of Korean life. What a shame. What a loss. However, I do not wish hardship on anyone and it seems to live in this country means certain hardship. I stand beside an old woman, stooped to half her height from relentless labor, her story indelibly marked on her face and body. Contrasted with the young woman on the other side of me, who is polished, shiny, unblemished, westernized to a startling degree. Even her mother language, her speech is liberally infused with Konglish, Korean English: computer, coca-cola, Bush, Clinton, New Kids on the Block, pronounced like a true red white and blue American-influenced Seoulite.

_6

What can I say now that I am back in the country I was born in, the country I lived in almost seven years, but now find it as foreign as anyone who grew up in the homogenous Midwest? I feel no connection to this place as of yet. I cannot speak Korean. I had hoped the language would have spilled out from the dark crevices of my memory, not forgotten after all, but dormant. And much like after a long winter, given a bit of light and a steady stream of speech, my tongue would conform to the phonetic based language. Instead I am tongue-tied and too self-conscious to speak: I look like one of them, but I am an outsider, an imposter. It is as though I have never spoken this language.

13

Omma and I sit together on the leather couch in the living room. She has just returned from her home in Ansan. I am unclear as to why she left in the first place.

Oppa and eonni left after talking to her at length, giving instructions is the best I could make of the one-sided conversation. I am certain I understand even less Korean than I did a week ago. This language will not seep in, which baffles me. Korean used to be my language. Why is it not coming back to me? Could it be a lack of desire to learn the language?

My family would be hurt if they thought I didn't want to learn their language. I'm not sure how I will get to know them without learning it. This language barrier is what prevents us from a deeper understanding of each other. By not learning Korean they might wrongly presume I don't want to get to know them.

Maybe it's explanation number two: I'm too lazy to learn. Although, if I use lazy as my excuse, I can do something about my energy level, I'm able to change that, goes my sound reasoning. I think I'll go with option three. I don't have the gift, the smarts for learning a new language.

Omma interrupts my ruminations over my lack of intelligence for language learning, she who can speak some Japanese, as well as basic Chinese. I clearly missed out on the linguistic gene.

"We go to you born village," Omma says as if we have been sitting here, had a conversation on this topic, weighed the pros and cons, and she has just now made her final decision. None of which we have done.

"What?"

"You born village. You born time. We go see."

We are going to the village where I was born. For a moment I am thrown off guard. I was born some place? I was born in a village? I kind of thought I was born at six years old. I mean, I *know* I wasn't, but without any memories before six, no photographs to document the event or baby pictures for proof, I had not contemplated the particulars of my birth, of being a baby.

But the events of getting on and off an airplane that was similar to a bird represented my momentous birth; the sky bird expelled me from its opening and plopped me down at the Minneapolis-St. Paul airport. Believe me, the story of storks delivering babies to parent's front door—think the movie, *Dumbo,* one of the first movies I saw after my arrival—was not all that much of a stretch for me.

"I don't remember being a baby."

"You pretty baby. Ipo. Pretty baby…. I show you…but wait for Oppa," Omma says, wiping away a tear.

Oppa and eonni return from the market laden with packages. Eonni has bought fresh crabs for dinner along with all the ingredients for a fire igniting spicy noodle dish that is Oppa's favorite. It will be so nuclear hot the girls will wince while trying small mouthfuls. I will find I cannot get enough of the stuff. It is a dish only Omma can make to Oppa's satisfaction. Oppa's arms are loaded with liquor of all sorts; beer, soju, and scotch. It looks like a party tonight at Oppa's house.

After a short conversation with Oppa, Omma disappears into Ah Hee's and Ah Rim's bedroom, the room they share during her stay. She returns with a shoebox under her arm. Oppa and I are sitting on the floor at a low table used for eating, or in this case, for drinks and ashtrays.

Omma has brought this box from her home in Ansan. Maybe that is why she went back to her place, to retrieve this box. Inside are black and white photographs. Omma has kept them in this shoebox all these years. I start sifting through the photographs. It does not dawn on me immediately that I am looking at myself. There are a handful of pictures of me at four or five years old wearing a hanbok, dancing. I stare at the pictures, glance up at Omma.

"Is this me?"

"Oh, sure, you young time. You ipo."

"Oh, my god...this is me...."

I cannot stop gazing at this happy little girl who looks to be imitating some sort of Korean dance. With her arms out, hands curved, head bent she sways to one side, as if in mid pose of some ancient dance she has seen not so long ago. If I line up these photos I can see her dance.

There are several more pictures of her/me in another *hanbok*, looking about a year older. This is the hanbok I brought with me from Korea. "Oh, I'm dancing the same way I did when I wore my hanbok for show and tell." I look at Omma. She has a radiant smile on her face, making her look ten years younger.

In these photographs I dance in an open space, a courtyard. I remember that courtyard! The courtyard from my childhood with its high walls and a gate locked only at night. This is where we lived with two other families each with their own house, the courtyard a common area.

I remember sitting up on the wall in the courtyard. For some reason, I was not supposed to be up there. I watched a line of people making their way to the gate. Most were elderly. They had their hands out begging for food. An old woman pulled her hair out, ground it in the dusty road and then collapsed. I screamed and screamed. Someone grabbed me off the wall and hustled me back into the house. I remember I kept crying. I'm surprised at this memory. Simply seeing the courtyard and the gate triggered this seemingly insignificant memory.

There are several photographs of me with a beehive hair-do. In one photograph Omma and I sport identical dos in what I think might have been a two for one hairstyle deal. Her beehive hair-do is covered by a light scarf tied under her chin. She wears a car coat with a white faux fur collar. Her hands are in her coat pockets. I stand next to her with hands in my pockets as if to imitate my mother's mannerisms. I am laughing.

There are several pictures of me on my first birthday. In Korean years it would be my second birthday. Koreans believe the day you are born you are one; that makes them always a year older. I have straight bangs across my forehead and the tiniest pigtails I have ever seen. I have fat cheeks and a double chin. I wear a beautifully stitched jacket with a small bow under my chins. I'm seated at a table that is covered with food. In the foreground are some nonfood items: a truck with candy in the cab bed, shoes, gold rings, a writing tablet, a small pile of Korean money, and a hanbok neatly folded on top of a box.

Omma explains it is customary to celebrate a child's second birthday. It was not so long ago that children often did not survive to their second birthday. Due to harsh living conditions, it was something of a miracle to survive that first year. Koreans believed if a child could make it to their second birthday, the spirits must have forgotten to snatch the child away. Grateful parents celebrate this momentous milestone.

The second part of the celebration is to see what the child's destiny is to be. The child is placed in front of various artifacts such as money and pencils. Omma claimed Oppa reached for money and that is why he has his own business and is rich, according to her.

As Omma is telling me about this custom, I wonder what I grabbed? Food? Eating is my hobby. Air? I mean, I have accomplished zero up to this point. Omma said I grabbed pencils, which symbolized either a scholar (no way) or writer. *Well there goes that lovely sentimental custom, it's full of holes.* I wanted to write, but I did not believe I had the talent for it.

In every picture, I am clearly happy. I cannot stop looking at this little girl in her various poses. This is Anny, I mean, ME! I am Anny. As I continue to comprehend this, a strange feeling comes over me. My heart opens and swells much like Dr. Seuss's The Grinch whose heart grows three sizes. Mine seems to be expanding just as large. I am proud to gaze upon this little girl. I am proud of her happy countenance shining back at the camera. I am proud that this little girl is me. That is my face. Those are my furrowed eyebrows. Whenever the sun shines on me I squint in a way that makes my eyebrows scrunch as if I'm annoyed, angry. It really is me.

"I was sooo cute!"

My family has a good laugh at my less than modest remark.

"You, ipo, pretty, pretty girl," Omma says again in her matter of fact way. "Everybody say you pretty. We go to beauty shop, everybody say 'ipo'. We wait at bus stop, 'oh, your little girl so pretty,' everybody say," Omma says to me, stressing the collective "everybody," which buffers the bragging and high opinions of a mother.

In another photograph I sit on the floor eating, of course, and I can just make out a man's foot in checkered socks. "Is this my father?" I ask, excited. Omma looks at me, startled. But no, it cannot possibly be my father. He left before I was born, never to be seen again. This person in the photograph is a family friend.

⸺ᦒ

Omma lets me take the photographs to my room. She tells me I can have any or all of them, if I want. It is late but I cannot stop staring at Anny. I mean, *me.* Even in the black and white photographs I can see my hair is not the black hair of most Koreans. It is sun streaked, with lighter strands that frame my face; the rest of my hair is medium brown.

In one photograph I am petting a dog. The dog looks at the camera as if to say, *I'll put up with this for about 30 seconds.* I am clearly smitten with him. There are pictures of me dressed in pretty dresses, clothes of all kinds. I can imagine Omma had fun dressing me. In almost every photograph I smile and pose for the camera. This is one happy child.

I cannot get enough of gazing at these pictures. I continue to stare at the adorable girl who dances in the courtyard. I wonder if Omma had decided by then to put me up for adoption. I thought back to the report my dad gave me about all the Amerasian babies that were outcasts in this society. I asked Omma about this. "Did people shun me, and you, because I was half Caucasian?"

Omma was startled by my question. "No, no, nobody say nothing, no difference to them." This was a non-issue in the tiny rural village where I lived.

In another photograph my hair is elaborately made up, probably with a hairpiece, curled and piled on top of my head. I have on the hanbok I brought to Minnesota. My right side is turned slightly toward the camera, my hand held in an unnatural pose. That hand lightly touches the sash on my hanbok jacket. The background, a painted land scape. I stand on a diamond pattern linoleum floor. I look like a quintessential Korean girl sitting for a professional picture. I believe this photo was taken days before I left.

Then there is the picture of Omma, Oppa and me. We stand in front of a brick building. It must be the orphanage. I am wearing the dress and tennis shoes I wore to Minnesota. My hair is piled in a coiffed bun on my head. I wear pearl earrings and hold the yellow purse. There is that cold sore on the left corner of my mouth and a scowl on my face. Omma, with short hair, has a grim expression. Oppa wears a cap, a white shirt. We look unhappily into the camera. This is the last photograph of us, probably taken hours before I left Korea.

I cry for what seems a long time, as quietly as I can.

Once I'm cried out, I sit up on my bed, wide awake. I cannot help but compare the newly discovered pictures I just looked through, with the photographs of my family and I back in Minnesota. Every so often my parents would get out the film projector or slide projector and we'd reminisce over the good old days.

Dad always started from the beginning when he and mom married, with mom in the beautiful wedding gown she made. AnnMarie would wear this same dress years later for her graduation ceremony at a private boarding school out east, where tradition dictated graduating seniors don an all white dress. The next series of photographs were of my parent's honeymoon at Niagra Falls. Then came the hundreds of pictures of Peter, clearly the first born child. It seemed most of the pictures were taken in the winter. We look at approximately three pictures of Tim, which he grumbled about, being the middle child, the overlooked child. AnnMarie has quite a few too, presumably the last child, and a girl.

I am the last to come up on the screen. Dad is teaching me how to ride a red bike, with training wheels, and then later without. My first Halloween dressed as a witch, eyebrows heavily blackened, black satin hat and cape. My baptism. Tim and I playing "wedding." I'm wearing my favorite dress with the pink sash, of course, and on my head I have on a white veil of sorts. Tim is serious in his role as the groom, in a navy blue blazer and *cape,* in imitation of prince charming. For years, whenever the kissing scene came on, Tim would rush out of the room, mortified.

In photograph after photograph I smile, beam, vamp for the camera, until I stopped. At eight or nine, I decided I did not want to look Korean anymore. In a Christmas photograph my siblings and

I are in front of the Christmas tree, they with their smiles. My face is screwed into a big scowl, eyebrows almost touching, my mouth pulled down in an over-exaggerated frown. I try to pull off what looks like an Elvis impersonation, my top lip snarled like Elvis's. In another photograph, on my eighth or ninth birthday, again a pouty mouth, furrowed brows. My arms crossed to emphasize a disgruntled attitude, in case my face did not convey that well enough.

While my siblings conjured up beatific smiles, my elastic countenance was evidence of a girl trying to alter her appearance the only way she could. But this unsophisticated girl did not see that, instead, her scrunched up face translated into an *absurd and ridiculous Korean face*. But I was amused by my face-altering elasticity. I was convinced it distracted the viewer from the obvious, that they saw me as a silly face-making girl and did not notice I was Korean. I was convinced I barely looked Korean when I made these faces.

In the quiet of night, photographs from my childhood spread out on the bedspread, I gaze at the little girl I once was. In almost every picture I grin and smile at the camera.

The next night, we gather around the same table to continue unraveling the years. I look at Oppa and see a quick flash of a smile at something Omma said. His face reposes to the handsome one I know, his smile never lingering. He has a solemn countenance, one that relays nothing until you look closely and see the pain and difficult times flit across his almond shaped eyes.

"Oppa say you have questions for him," Omma says, looking at Oppa and back at me. "He think you have something you want to say."

I wonder how he knows this, but I sense Oppa is a good judge of people. He seems to observe and take in, rather than do and react, which is my style.

"I do have something to say. I don't know how to say it." I want to choose my words carefully. "I'm…I, I forgot you. I'm sad that I forgot you, Oppa. How could I have forgotten you?" I sniffle, trying to hold back my tears. So much for carefully crafted words.

Omma starts to translate my words to Oppa, but he stops her. He understands what I have said. There is a long silence as Oppa takes in what he has heard. Eonni and my nieces look distressed, Omma dabs at her eyes.

"I'm so sorry," I say, looking at Oppa.

Eonni, Oppa, and Omma speak at once. I understand none of it. They stop and try to take turns speaking, but they cannot wait for the other to finish. They look at me anxiously.

"Oppa think it big surprise to you"—

"Anny," Oppa interrupts, "little girl, he puts out his hand to demonstrate me at about two feet tall, "little girl," he says emphatically. He chokes on his words and looks at Omma, nods to her to go on.

"You so young. You scared, maybe. You forget fast, you have new life. Forget old life," Omma says, choking on the last words.

I look at each of them, my family. Again, tears take over.

⁶

A photograph of Oppa and me: I'm about three, he's twelve or thirteen. We're sitting on a low curb and even though there is ample space around us, we are smashed together as if we want to be in each other's skin. It is obvious we are content, as only innocent children can be when their world seems right. "Oppa, you *taegi*, fat little boy," I say teasingly. He smiles and laughs. I do like hearing his laughter.

I could do no wrong in Oppa's eyes. I was his little sister and he was at my mercy. He would drop whatever he was doing whenever

I called for him. If he received a treat, he always shared it with me, giving me the bigger portion. He and Omma spoiled me ridiculously.

How is it I forgot my brother? I turn this over in my mind. I search my hazy memories for a glimpse of him behind a tree, around a building, beyond the railroad tracks near our home. He is nowhere.

Oppa understands the depth of my memory loss. He understands. He has given me permission to forgive myself. He understands that sometimes a memory is too much for a young girl to keep when she cannot have her big brother with her. She could not bear the pain of no longer having him in her new life. She wills herself to bury the memories of him, to forget him. To bear the crush of loss, it is best to believe he never existed. It hurts a little less this way.

It is now past midnight, but no one is sleepy. We are too wound up from retelling and reliving our pasts. I mention again the non-existent younger brother that Oppa and I discussed in our first telephone conversation. Omma is surprised by the news. Oppa cannot understand how there could be false information in my adoption papers. They both shake their heads. There was no younger brother.

All these years, I thought I had a younger brother. Omma and Oppa continue to shake their heads. There was no such child.

It is amazing what the mind can imagine if given time and a bit of information, or misinformation. It can create a different history. It can create fiction all its own. I am sure psychologists would have a field day with me, my lack of memories. Perhaps there is information available on how the brain splits in two when a child is separated from her family. How she must shut out memories, accept others' words on documents, and create characters and scenes to fit the script. I believe there is a whole psychological buffet of issues I can learn from books, counseling, if I feel so inclined. But it is being here with my family that is the best medicine.

14

Instead of going with us on our nightly walk, Oppa has shut himself off in his room for the last hour or so. I hear mournful old-time Korean songs coming from his stereo. The song, the instrumentals grate on my nerves. Even though I have no idea what the actual words are, it sounds gratuitously melancholy and forlorn. Every once in a while he tries to sing along, but his voice breaks with emotion, unable to continue. He lets the singer sing on, about her bad luck life with no good in sight as she clings to her lover as he leaves. It sounds like a Korean version of a country western song, of loss, bottomless sorrow.

Omma and I sit on the green leather couch. My nieces and eonni sit on the floor. They watch some game show in a language I still am unable to grasp. I don't want to watch TV. I'm wondering why Oppa has closed himself off, drinking Soju and singing-crying sad songs by himself. Each time he sings along eonni looks at me and gives a nervous laugh. She pulls down her mouth into an exaggerated sad face, while pointing to her heart and pantomiming that Oppa hurts here. I nod my head acknowledging that I understand. But I have no idea the depth of his sadness. I only see the now, of a brother who has clearly done well for himself, having created his own printing company, lives in an upwardly mobile area of Seoul. By most people's standards he has *made it*.

Yet I see in him, and with older Korean people in general, a mountain of sadness and hurt, buried deep. A sorrow that might have been the demise of a lesser people, but taciturn Koreans forged on, railed against their suffering, built up their country, exported steel, surely a metaphor of their strength, while tamping down their pain. But look past the surface and into the eyes of anyone alive around the time of the Korean War, and in the aftermath, see the shadows of dark times that mark a nation. That is Oppa's face.

"Anny, come here," he calls from his room. I'm relieved, eager to be in his presence. He sits cross-legged on the floor in gray and blue boxer shorts, a white undershirt, with a cigarette in his mouth, a glass of Soju in his hand. He pats the yellow cushion next to him, gestures for me to sit. I try to sit cross-legged, but I must have a wall or some kind of backrest, my westernized body cannot support itself without it. It's another blatant reminder of my Korean inabilities. I pull away from the wall convinced I can sit like a real Korean this time. I am desperate to prove to my family I haven't turned completely American.

"It's okay, your back, no good," he says and smiles. He is giving me permission to be comfortable over custom. I smile gratefully at him. I marvel at his understanding. Though his Korean *doenseng* has been replaced by an American one he accepts me the way I am. His smile fades and he looks at me solemnly.

"Anny, I had examinations to study for, so I could not come home to you and Omoni for my weekend visit. I was the top student in my class. My teacher was proud of me and he expected me to do well. I did not want to disappoint him or Omoni. I stayed at Aunt's house longer than I normally do. You can imagine then how anxious I was to see you. It was the longest train ride! I believe the train was taunting me, it knew I wanted to be home, to be with you and Omoni. Imagine my surprise when the train drew near our village and I did not see you. That was a first, since you always met me. But when I did not see Omoni waiting, I became alarmed. I thought she had fallen ill, or you had. I jumped off the train and never touched the ground until I was home. Inside I found Omoni in a corner of the house. You were nowhere. She had been crying for a long time, perhaps all day. I asked her what was wrong. I asked where you were. This made her cry all the more. She could not get the words out. I was frightened. I had never seen Omoni fall apart like this. I sat with her until at last she was calm enough to speak.

I could not take in what she was saying. Orphanage? America? Two days? Every time Omoni said something, my mind could not absorb it. I could only repeat her incomprehensible words.

You were in an orphanage you'd been there for many days now. You were being prepared for adoption. That meant getting your shots, your vaccinations; they were teaching you some English; and they had you eating American-style food. Omoni visited you every day. She thought she could bring you home the last days, but they would not let her. We had one day and one night left with you. We would be leaving for Seoul early the next morning.

I felt like I was drowning, Anny. It felt as though I was deep under the sea in the darkest place, held down by things I could not name.

I do not remember the rest of that day, night, or how we got to the orphanage the next morning. It was a terrible last day. Omoni and I found you sitting in the main office. You were small for six, but because you were scared and sickly, you looked even smaller. You had a bad sore on the corner of your mouth. It would heal—probably nerves, they said. The rest of the day is lost on me. But that night, in the tiny room we stayed in, the last night together as a family, I knew what I had to do. I was going to bring you back. I could not keep you from going, I had no power to do that, but I would bring you back some day. But how? I was only sixteen. How could I possibly do this? That is what I pondered all night.

The dreaded morning came quickly. Have you noticed time speeds up all the more when you no longer want to see another day? None of us slept. You looked like you had lost the other half of yourself over night, so thin, unable to keep food down, weepy and frightened. We could not eat and we had nothing to say. They took a picture of us. Omoni made sure you looked your best; had your hair done at a beauty salon; bought a new dress for you, with pearl earrings and a purse; along with a note to your new family, blessing them and asking them to take good care of you.

We arrived at Kimpo Airport. The place was crowded and chaotic: grown-ups were panicky and upset, children, crying. But I needed to tell you my plan before it was too late. I could see I did not have much time. I took you aside, to the quietest spot, even though the American lady said no. I had to tell you so you could keep these words for yourself. I knelt down in front of you and, while holding your hand, I said to you, *Anny, I promise you three things I will do with my life: I am going to own my own company. I will become rich and when I have enough money, I will find you and I will bring you back to Korea.* I said my promises to you again, to make sure you would not forget. And then they took you away.

A broken brother and sister unleash a volcanic eruption of grief, of pent-up loss. Boundaries of time, of language, of replaced family, and lands separated by oceans, cave in. Swimming against the current of pasts torn apart, brother and sister fold into one another and fill the divide. Tears wash over them, melding and wending down their Asian faces, necks, onto their clothes, intertwined fingers. Cradling each other, two grieving siblings find their way back.

Oppa and I lie spent on the floor. The house is silent. The songs are long over and the rest of the family is asleep in the living room. My swollen eyes feel raw to the touch. I have a continuous runny nose my short sleeves are wet from wiping it. Yet amazingly, I feel lighter, an instant weight loss program for the soul. I look at Oppa with his shiny tear-stamped face and he too seems surprised by the effect of this telling. I cannot make sense of this new sensation. It will take time to feel less heavy, to have more room, like expanding a house to make space, filling it with precious and even frivolous tokens of who we are.

He has pulled a small piece of paper out of his wallet. It is a business card. He hands it to me without a word; he is unable to speak. On the paper in English are the words *Korean Social Service*. There is an address. It is the agency that handled my adoption. They are affiliated with Lutheran Social Service in Minnesota. Together they worked to transform me from a poor Korean girl into an American one. I hand it back to Oppa. I think this is one memento I don't want. He doesn't readily take it back. With my hand out itching to get rid of it, he tells me he has kept the address of this agency in his wallet for twenty-two years. It was his daily reminder of his promises to me. He wanted the address available for when the time was right.

Oppa had to quit school about the time I left. There was no money for him to continue. In Korea there are no public schools where one can get a free education. He was sixteen when he told his teacher he could no longer continue his schooling. His teacher wept. Oppa was his top student. Instead he became an apprentice at a printing shop where he learned every facet of the business. He worked tirelessly until he acquired his own company.

⁓

I have learned my way around a small section of Seoul. One direction in particular has become familiar to me since Oppa often drives that same route from his apartment complex. Outside the apartment maze, off a newly constructed four-lane street, is a small park with hills and paths. It's probably two miles from the apartment. So I have decided to resume jogging like I did back home.

But Omma thought this was a bad idea the first time I mentioned it to her. She believed I would get lost. She wanted to come with me. "You're going to run?" I asked her.

"No, no, I walk." That was not going to work. I promised her I knew my way back. But each time I ran, she followed me as far as she could until I left her behind with a wave. As I finished my run and rounded the corner on Oppa's street, there she was pacing back and forth. When she saw me, it was as if the sun broke through gray clouds.

No one runs in Seoul. This fitness craze, to run outside on the sidewalks of Seoul, has not yet caught on. Yet most people I pass do not think twice of a Korean-looking girl jogging. At the park, a few of the *Halmonis*, grandmas, think it fun to run beside me a few steps, to experience what this westernized Korean girl is doing. They do not go far. They stop, throw up their hands, shake their heads at this ridiculous activity. I laugh with them when they realize it is not that enjoyable. They wave me off as if to say, *ah, youth and your western ways.* Others watch momentarily and then resume whatever they are doing.

I'm eager to listen to U2's, *Achtung, Baby,* a cassette that I bought recently at Lotte Department store. I slip the tape into my Walkman, reassure Omma I'll be back soon, and ignore her as she walks out with me and down the street.

Running is the only thing I know how to do in this foreign land. I am helpless here. Most of the time I feel like a dependent child, relying on my family for every little and big thing. I cannot speak the language. I do not know the customs, how to behave. I'm sure I've made countless daily faux pas. Plus I'm used to living alone. Never have my living quarters been this close, not even with my family back home.

Running offers not only an endorphin rush for my body and mind but also an hour of respite for me, and, perhaps for my family, as well.

I run up the flight of stairs to the park. U2's *End of the World* is pulsating in my ears. And then, a thought comes to mind about last summer before my auspicious news. That *sensation* I did not understand. That semi-conscious awareness *something* was going to happen that came and went all summer. It disappeared at about the time of the news of my Korean family's search. With the excitement of reconnecting with my family, I did not give it any thought, but now it comes back to me. I remember. I turn off the tape. A large craggy rock which overlooks a small section of the city is off to the right. I climb up on it.

That sensation. That was Anny/me remembering. Somewhere in her/my sub conscious I remembered Oppa. My sense memory remembered the promise he made to me. *He would find me and bring me back to Korea.*

I think back to that night of the telephone call from my mom. The shock I experienced. How I watched myself become two selves. The *bemused* self hovered above looking down at the *stunned* self on the wooden floor. Her expression seemed to say she had been expecting this very news. As though in the last twenty-two years since my adoption this had been in the realm of possibilities. The weighted me on the floor, however, was unable to process the bizarre words, and, instead, continued to stare at the knowing me.

That *knowing* part of me remembered Oppa. Remembered the sensation of his words, his promise. I held those words in my memory, in my deepest layer of memory. I did not forget him. I was waiting for him to find me. I had always been waiting for him. Just like he promised. It had been the universe's way of telling me to hold on.

15

"Anny, we go," Omma said to me this morning. This now comes to mean I go without comment. I used to ask where we were going, but now I know better. I have to be selective about my questions. It's overwhelming and exhausting to hear broken English and Korean strung together, with a hefty dose of inference for some semblance of understanding. I'm saving my questions and any other important conversations for later, it's only mid-morning.

I am dressed like I always dress, that is to say, shabbily, by Korean standards. In Minnesota I'd fit right in, but for Seoul, I am under dressed—all the time. Korean women do not step out of their houses without the full makeup routine, hair in place, dress and heels, just to go to market for fish or vegetables or fixings to make kimchi.

I'm wearing shorts and a sleeveless blouse I bought in one of Seoul's cheapest shops, I presume, by the way eonni turned up her nose when she felt the material while inspecting the blouse. It will probably shrink after the first wash, and it needs one hot iron to get the creases out, but I like the pattern, the colors, cranberry red and moss green.

I look at Oppa in his gray green suit. Omma has on a nice blue and white blouse with matching white cotton sweater and navy skirt. She even has a touch of lipstick on. I am seriously under dressed for wherever we are going.

I need a minute to change, I tell Oppa. The problem is I do not have any nice clothes. I am a waitress. I hang out in smoky bars and walk or bike everywhere I go. I like to think my clothes say casual. I think in eonni's eyes I am one cheap shirt away from beggar. She looks at me, disappointed, everytime I come out dressed for the day.

I put on a dressy blue T-shirt I bought at Dayton's long ago, along with a peasant style skirt that has the same light blue as the shirt. To my dismay, it makes me look ten pounds heavier.

It's hard to believe I was once a girl who cared about her clothes and appearance. I wonder where she went? In my former life I used to pride myself in knowing the distinct styles of Valentino, Michael Kors, and Japanese designers that are long absent from my vocabulary. I know eonni would find that hard to believe.

About half way to our destination Omma mentions my best friend from the village. Do I remember her? I do not. This question comes out of nowhere. Why is she asking about a best friend that I used to have? Is Omma trying to make small talk? She does not make small talk, I've noticed. No one talks unless they have to. We're a pretty quiet bunch.

Oppa stops at a nondescript store, or at least I think it's a store. I have come to learn Koreans' concept of aesthetics does not often extend to store fronts or interiors. Omma and I wait in the car. Oppa reappears holding a small plastic jewelry box. Inside, a tiny 18-carat gold ring on red velvet. It is too small for any of us or even for my nieces. It is for a baby. Omma tells me it is for my best friend's baby boy.

"What? What best friend?" I say, baffled.

"You no remember Young Mi? You best friends," Omma says. I have no memory of her.

"You scratch her face, right here," Omma says, as she demonstrates with her finger a long gash mark down her left cheek.

"What? Why did I do that?" I say, sitting up, completely attentive to this new piece from my past.

"No sweat, she do to you too," Omma says. She points to my right cheek. "She scratch you, she do that." She turns back to the front seat. There's nothing more to say. Then she remembers something else and turns to me, but instead, begins to laugh at my expression, my mouth hanging open in surprise.

It happened long ago. We fought about something. "No problem," Omma says, "they not mad at you." Supposedly all is forgiven and forgotten. Apparently that goes double for me, the forgetting, at least. I cannot picture this girl who was my best friend and someone I fought. I have no idea who she is or what she looks like. But what Omma says is correct, at least about the mark on my cheek. I have a faint V shaped scratch on my right cheek. I never would have believed it was from my best friend, a best friend I do not remember.

My former best friend lives in an unremarkable building, like so many sprouting up in Seoul. We take the elevator. I am struck by the oddity of this moment. I have no idea who this supposed best friend is. I feel at a disadvantage. She and my family have been able to keep their memories alive over the years by getting together to reminisce and rehash the events. While eating and drinking I imagined they laughed when retelling of Anny scratching Young Mi, and how Young Mi, not putting up with it, did a turn on Anny. They can recount the events that led up to it and what they did afterwards. They can continue telling stories of the next twenty-three years in the same place, with the same people, in their common language.

She is prepared for this reunion. I am not.

I'm dwelling on these mixed feeling as we arrive at Young Mi's apartment. Oppa rings the buzzer. The door opens and there stands a woman my age. I gasp. I do not recognize her, except that she has a noticeable gash on her cheek. This is my handiwork, or rather, my fingernail work. She could not forget me even if she wanted to, not with that mark as a daily reminder.

She gives me a demure smile and welcomes us in. I know I am rude, staring at her deformed cheek. *I must have been very mad to leave that kind of mark.* She ignores my unblinking, open-mouthed stare, takes me by the hand, and leads me into her house.

"Young Mi welcomes you to her house. Long time no see," Omma says, surely paraphrasing her words.

"Tell her thank you for inviting us to celebrate her son's birth," I look again at her scar, "and tell her I'm so sorry for what I did to her."

"She say, no sweat, no worry, come and eat."

We sit on the floor of my former best friend's living room. I catch a glimpse of her husband at one point, in another room with the TV on, surrounded by his family, I presume. She brings out her extremely chubby baby and we coo at how healthy and adorable he is. A chubby baby is what every good Korean mother strives to achieve, which signifies a healthy one.

The rest of the visit is spent with people, talking and sitting and nibbling on watermelon. I am not included in the conversation, and because Koreans rarely make eye contact, I have no idea, until later, that I am the main topic of conversation. I only understand the conversation when Omma's honorary uncle, who knew my father, remarks that we both have similar shaped mouths, particularly the upper lip. He draws the shape of my upper lip in the air, and others comment, point at their mouth, point at mine, others draw the shape in the air as they discuss the similarities. My mouth is not unique, so it surprises me that this ordinary feature is worth discussion. The most surprising is to discover my mouth is similar to my father's mouth.

Some of these people were once a part of my life. Yet none is familiar to me. I search my diminished memory trying to remember my childhood days. There are only brief snippets, a blur of colors and shapes, vague images, none of it creates a story. And none of these snatches of scenes, moments in time, include a best friend. This bothers me. But it also explains how I can easily move on, how I rarely look back or keep in touch with former friends. Much like at the end of a movie after the credits roll and the screen faded to black, what do you do? You walk out of the theater and resume your life.

There was no more Korea. No more Omma. No more Oppa. No more people that made up that life. A new film began with a new script, new actors, scenes. No use dwelling on the previous footage, it's difficult to retell in a new language you have yet to master. Once you do, you cannot remember who the actors were, or what the story was about. Who wants to hear a story when you cannot remember the details?

⁓

Several days ago Omma said we would go to my *born village*. I have come to understand the limitations of Omma's English. Past and future tenses are nonexistent. It all takes place now. So a few nights ago when she mentioned *we go to your born village* that could have meant in a day or three months from now. It looks like it is today.

The drive out of Seoul is supposed to take about an hour, but the traffic crawls along, bumper to bumper, all day, everyday. Once out of Seoul, it's less congested and I am relieved to be out in open land with mountains in the distance.

The first thing I see is the abandoned American army base. It is surprisingly small. Without asking what it is, I know it was once a base, the high walled fortress a give-away. This is where my American father and Omma met. I look away. We continue on a short distance.

The railroad tracks. These are the tracks from my childhood. The train had been the lifeline of our lives, central in my dim memory.

Now I know these are the tracks that brought Oppa home from school. On the few occasions we went to Seoul, we took the train from here. Did my father leave from these tracks?

The village itself is not really a village, as far as I can see. It is more of a small compound. Newly constructed concrete walls are being built to house a communal space big enough for several families, or extended families to live in. Amazingly, some of the same people from my childhood still live here.

We have lunch with Omma's friend. I find out later she took care of me when I was a baby. She is in her underground kitchen preparing our lunch, Omma tells me to come take a look.

This kitchen is down a short flight of stairs on the outside of her small house. The stove is in a cellar-like space under the house used not only for cooking, but also for heating the floor of the living space above. I remember a kitchen similar to this one that was ours. How it heated the upper room, and as a little girl, I slept in the corner on the linoleum floor, a spot blackened from the heat of the stove. I remember the sensation of warmth on my little girl body. How I curled up like a cat and felt warm and safe. I am surprised that this memory has come to light at this moment.

We sit down to a simple meal of fish soup, rice and root vegetables that are abundant in the area. It is all delicious. Omma's friend has given us the best that she has. There are many bows and grateful *kamsahamnidas* and the honorific *kamsahashimnika* for her hospitality.

Someone takes a picture of the three of us out on the tracks. In the background are agricultural buildings and green houses. Oppa and I flank Omma. While Oppa seems to smile, I feel too pained to force anything beyond a minimal effort. Omma attempts a half-hearted smile. *My born village.*

16

The night after our return from the village, I say to Oppa I am beginning to recall an unformed memory. It is perhaps something unpleasant from my childhood. This image hovers over me like Korea's summer humidity: there is no escaping it. I am remembering something strange about the railroad tracks. That I feared those tracks…I see myself waiting for someone…I think this person was going to hurt me….

Oppa takes in my solemn face. He listens quietly and I can see his mind at work. Oppa tells Omma, who did not come in with us after our nightly walk, wanting instead to enjoy a cigarette out in the quiet neighborhood, that a memory is coming back to me. Omma is visibly upset, but she does not press me for information.

Eonni lays the ubiquitous *ojinga, soju*, cigarettes, and watermelon out on the low table where we sit Korean style on the floor. Due to the gravity of this faint memory that confuses me, Oppa wants to get to the matter at hand, to the heart of the memory. It is not even a memory, really, just quick images that make no sense. There is a man I fear for some reason. He might have abused me. He has a clean-shaven head, wears a cap. Omma and I wait for someone on a train. There is some sort of commotion while waiting for this person. I see a man getting off the train, and then he seems to be almost buried by the crush of people, of women, I think. They seem to consume him. In the next scene, I'm firmly led by this man as we walk to a house, a door closes….

"I think I might have been abused," I say, nervous at the thought of potentially opening up a pandora's box. I look at Omma as she translates my words to Korean. They talk over each other trying to sort out the story, the details of my images. It is taking longer than I expected. My head swings left, right, Oppa, Omma, Oppa, Omma, like watching a tennis match, the ball volleying back and forth back and forth. They want to make sure their story aligns and is accurate before they explain in English. Except, much to my surprise, they begin to laugh. They stop their collaborative recall mid exchange to laugh some more. I'm put off by their laughter, that they find humor in this grave situation. Abuse is hardly a laughing matter. I wait impatiently for the two of them to stop chuckling and explain, miffed that they find my serious memory humorous.

Omma stands at the railroad tracks looking down the line. Of course she does not see the train yet, she knows she is much too early, but she feels impatient and anxious, wishing the train to appear carrying her sixteen-year-old son.

She looks behind her, away from the direction the train will come. Yes, Anny is still there, some distance away. No amount of cajoling or demanding will bring her daughter to her side. Omma looks at her daughter's bent head and knows Anny is afraid too. She tries silently to will her daughter to look up at her, so she can give her some sort of assurance, but her daughter is lost in her thoughts, perhaps imagining the worst. What can a six-year-old girl possibly imagine the worst to be, Omma wonders, looking pitifully at her only daughter.

It was on these very tracks, before he left to continue living his life in America, she promised Anny's father she would give their unborn daughter the American name he requested. She hasn't thought about him in years, yet now she wonders how different it all would have been if she had gone with him, how she wouldn't be standing on the tracks waiting for her son to do what a husband, a father should do.

Omma has never doubted or questioned the ways of her patriarchal society. Her life has been marked by the confines and demands of her culture, first as a girl, then a woman and now, as a mother. Her part as a mother did not involve a man's duty: to correct and punish the wayward behaviors of her troublemaker daughter. But her son took his obligations seriously, or as seriously as a sixteen-year-old boy could, away at school during the week, returning only on a rare weekend. Up until now, his duties as the man of the house were unremarkable. Today, the people of this small village will bear witness to whether he will be able to keep his little sister in line.

But it is her spirited daughter that concerns her. Omma knows she cannot say no to Anny. She cannot remember a time she has. She dotes on her daughter, crossing far outside the line of good parenting by needlessly spoiling her.

Omma ruminates on what Oppa might do to Anny once he is told the trouble she has caused in the village. He loves her as much as Omma does. Wasn't it Anny he grabbed and whose shoulders he sobbed into the first week he was to be apart from them? Wasn't it Anny Oppa's eyes searched for in the crowd greeting the weekend train? It was Anny who could pull him away from his studies to play with her out in the courtyard. And it was Anny, Oppa readily hugged and held for too long until she could take no more of his cloying, wriggling out of his arms and running free. His love for Anny, abundant, but unbeknownst to him he now is to be burdened with punishing her. Once he hears all the grievances against his sister, would he be filled with shame? Would his love for her change? What kind of punishment would he mete out?

Omma hears them first before she sees them. She looks in the direction of the wild noise, a cacophonic cackling rising into the air as The Angry Mothers ascend the low bank. To Omma they look like a brood of hens ready to drive out the innocent. Each Mother drags with her a sullen, reluctant child. As The Mothers gain on her, the squawking becomes indignant words directed at Omma: *Anny punched! Anny scratched! Anny bit! Anny!* Omma had heard these accusations before, as the exaggerated gossip spread and returned to her. It wasn't the tall-tales against her daughter that were upsetting, but the obvious and mean-spirited way each mother grabbed her child as Omma and Anny passed. It pained Omma to see her daughter ostracized.

The loud blast of the train's whistle jolts Omma back to reality. Her stomach leaps to her throat. *Anny. Anny!* Panic continues to rise as she scans the heads of The Mothers, looking for her frightened daughter. Omma's heart lurches as she sees her daughter standing alone, crying. The Mothers remain at a distance from her, as if she has leprosy, Omma thinks. A volcanic anger is ready to erupt, she wants to tell The Mothers exactly what she thinks of them, but she catches herself. She knows this will make matters worse for her daughter. She does the unbearable as a mother: she remains silent.

Anny! Oppa shouts and waves excitedly from the top step of the train, oblivious to what awaits him below. As he bounds down the steps thinking only of catching Anny and tossing her in the air as he often does, The Mothers move in. They surround the unsuspecting boy, grabbing and pulling on his shirtsleeve, his arms, any part they can latch on to, a tug of war for his full attention as they peck him with their accusations.

The Mothers want immediate justice. Anny is to be punished severely. The Mothers will accept nothing less. The Mothers offer suggestions, which to an outside observer suggest medieval times. Above the uproar, Oppa calls for Anny. The Mothers fall away to expose the lone chick among the wolves, all eyes on Anny. Omma catches a glimpse of her son, his face drained of color. She has never seen this look on her son's face before. *Aigoooo!* Omma cries out. This pleases

The Mothers, hearing the unmistakable sound of fear in Omma's voice.

Anny! COME HERE! Anny begins to whimper hearing her brother's angry command. On unsteady legs, she makes the short walk to her brother. He demands that she look up at him. She raises her heavy head, but cannot look into his darkened eyes. His words hurt her ears. *Shame to the family. Disappointed. Horrible child. Can't bear the sight of you.* She does not hear what her punishment is to be. She only hears the echo of his first words; words that mean that he no longer loves her.

Oppa tells the crowd of agitated mothers he will take care of this matter, his deep frown, an encouraging sign to The Offended Mothers. They are pleased. They approve, smiling smugly, nodding to one another. This will teach Anny a proper lesson, bring her down a notch in attitude, The Mothers whisper as they trail behind Oppa, Omma bringing up the rear.

Oppa stands at the entrance to their door waiting respectfully for Omma to enter first. The Mothers gather just outside the door to hear everything. After Omma is safely tucked inside, Oppa assures The Mothers he will hand out the punishment at once. He encourages The Mothers to go home and do what they do best—continue taking excellent care of their families. The Mothers, sated by his compliments, disband quickly to do just that.

Oppa ushers his trembling sister into the house. The door sticks, as if reluctant to close. No one will be able to bear witness to what Oppa will do. *Look at me,* he says. Frightened, she slowly raises her eyes, but suddenly, he scoops her up into the air and twirls her around. Meeting his gaze, Anny sees not an angry Oppa or a scary one. Instead, he smiles a joyful grin he reserves for her. He still loves her! Omma laughs and it catches Anny off guard. She looks from Oppa to Omma trying to understand what this means. Oppa laughs, and once Anny realizes he is not angry at her, she joins in. Once the laughter dies down, Oppa reaches for her. He gives her a hearty hug. Anny returns the hug, but this time, it is she who does not let go. She holds on tightly to her Oppa.

So Oppa had the duty of punishing me. It turns out I was often in trouble because I felt I could, and did, boss the other village children. I was the self-appointed leader of a ragamuffin band of boys and girls in the village. If these children didn't follow my ways, I scratched or bit them, I hit them into obedience. I was a one-girl regime of terror.

Oppa could never lay a hand to me. His love for me did not include spankings or slaps or any harshness. All he wanted was to hold me in the privacy of our house where no revenge-seeking mothers could observe what was happening behind the door. He played being pretend-mad, aggrieved by my actions, made promises of punishment for The Mothers' benefit. Oppa did not punish me; instead he indulged and maybe even spoiled me.

I was more fascinated by the fact that I was a naughty girl. "So, I was quite a little shit," I say, with pride. Yes, I was. I like Anny all the more for her feisty nature.

17

Oppa suggests to me that I go with him. It is late evening; I cannot imagine where we are going. It is still raining as it has all day, living up to its reputation as the monsoon season.

As we head out, Oppa grabs a large umbrella. He drives through an older section of Seoul onto a narrow street. Cars park halfway up on the sidewalk on this otherwise slim street that is difficult for passing cars to get through. He finds a spot to park, leaves the engine running. Up ahead I see people standing near a gate holding umbrellas and looking towards a building.

"Ah Young's school," Oppa says, before I have a chance to ask him the obvious. "She study late tonight."

More cars pull in near us. Parents get out holding sturdy umbrellas. They wait patiently for their daughters to finish their studies. As soon as the school doors open, parents rush to meet their daughters, to keep them dry in the downpour. As they walk past the car, I see mothers, fathers with arms protectively around their daughters.

For some reason, this gets me. Tears well up, a lump is lodged in my throat. I try to explain my tears to Oppa and Ah Young. They at first do not regard the specialness of this act.

"It's beautiful to see these loving gestures, of parents caring for their daughters in this simple way, " I say, trying to express the varying emotions I feel. It is not lost on me that once not so long ago Koreans did not value their daughter's learning as much as their son's. Parents regard a girl's education just as important as they do a boy's. More families now have the financial means to ensure their girls receive a fair opportunity to obtain that necessary education. "It's heart-warming," I say, wiping away my tears. Both Oppa and Ah Young seem to see this situation anew.

Oppa shakes his head, "Beautiful. Yes, beautiful." Ah Young smiles in agreement.

After dinner, Oppa and I go for a walk. I have been cooped up in the apartment most of the day with the air conditioning running continuously. I need fresh air though it is a humid night. Minnesota's humidity can be difficult to adjust to, but it is nothing compared to this. If you look at a map you see Korea and Minnesota are on the same latitude, except Korea, a peninsula is surrounded by water.

I'm hot and sticky before we get half way down the block. Regardless, it's enjoyable walking around with Oppa. We stop at the video store and rent some American movies. He likes horror flicks. He has seen most of them. He chooses Friday the Thirteenth. "You'll have to watch that one alone," I tell him. "I'm not fond of scary movies." He smiles and says it's not scary.

We slowly head back to Oppa's—I think. I don't know this area. We've gone a new way tonight, so I count on his guidance. We enjoy each other's company whether we talk or quietly walk hand in hand. But I've been thinking about Oppa and his responsibilities. "You have a great burden, Oppa, to provide for three girls, a wife, and Omma," I say, after walking some time in silence. My understanding of Korean culture is that the eldest son is responsible for caring for his mother.

"I wish for a boy," he says.

"You mean you're still trying for more children?"

"No, no," Oppa says, laughing, "No more."

I understand he means at one time he wished for a boy. I know boys are revered in this culture. I imagine it has crossed Oppa's mind, wanting a boy. Probably each time eonni was pregnant he might have prayed for one, although I suspect Oppa's not much for praying.

"Why don't you adopt a boy?"

"No, no. Korean people don't adopt."

"No kidding they don't adopt. That's why Omma had to send me off to the States. Because Korean people don't adopt their own. They don't want to contaminate their pure lineage." Oppa stops walking, he doesn't look at me, but faces in my direction. I know he doesn't understand every word I'm saying, but he's attentive to the change in my voice, rapid words.

"That's the problem with this country. That's the big shame, isn't it?" I say, angrily. "I remember during the Olympics, the government postponed all adoptions and considered doing so for good. But Korea can't end their adoptions, can they? So Americans and Europeans continue to take in Korea's cast-offs. Otherwise what will become of all the unwanted children since its own people refuse them?"

I'm hopping mad now. Oppa continues to stand and take in my haranguing.

"That's why I was sent to America. That's why our family is having a reunion. That's why I can't talk to you in my first language, why I know nothing about this culture, why I'm a foreigner and why Korea will never be my home." I'm crying. People look our way. Some stare. My agitated movements, my raised voice, tears, are difficult to ignore. Oppa looks at me straight-on.

"I hate this country for not taking care of all its people, for passing them off to other countries. Koreans need to take care of what's theirs." I say through tears. I'm surprised at my sudden impassioned feelings.

He takes in my fallen face, my sagged shoulders, tears rolling down my cheeks.

"Okay, Anny, I understand. I'm sorry."

I'm instantly ashamed of myself. Yelling at Oppa as if he is personally responsible for our situation, for the adoption plight, the customs of this country. "No, I'm sorry, Oppa. I'm sorry I yelled at you. It's not your fault. God, Oppa, it's not your fault." We walk the rest of the way home in silence.

～∽

How fortunate you are to be adopted. What good parents you have, people often said to me. *You have the world by the tail,* my grandma would say as a reminder to me if I was acting like an ingrate, and that I should be thankful to my folks for taking me in. For many, the positives of adoption were easy to enumerate: I escaped poverty, acquired a new family, an education, a possibility at a good future.

But how does one measure the value of adoption? What does one place on the scales? What is the weight of dispossession: of language, culture, identity, and family? What do I weigh on the other scale? Is it the opportunities of material acquisitions and societal achievements, accomplishments? What holds the greater value?

Before I left for Korea, a cousin tells me that he asked my dad how he felt, me reuniting with my family. My dad's reply was of joy, happiness for me; he has known I've had a hole in my heart, of sadness, a loss that seemed to grow. Years before, Ben expressed the same sentiment too.

Adoption is not for the faint-hearted; it is not a win-win or a lose-lose. It is somewhere in between. I will try to navigate between two worlds, straddle two countries, two cultures, two identities. I can be mad at a country, a government who ought to take better care of its people by giving help and support to women who find themselves in tough economic situations. By changing the attitude, the culture of exporting children to other countries, and creating systems within its own country to better children and women's lives is a good start.

But it is futile to ponder the *what ifs* and the *could have beens* though I am guilty of doing this. I am still adjusting to this monumental life shift. For now, I am trying to keep in mind that we have the extraordinary good fortune of reunion, a chance to know each other as adults. I feel grateful and blessed to connect with my family.

‑ɔ

Oppa pulls out the Korean Social Service business card I refused the other night. He tells me when he was finally ready to contact them, he discovered they had moved. It took some time to find their new location. Yet the original buildings and grounds are still in operation as a hospital for babies with special needs before they are sent to the orphanage.

He wants to see the orphanage that I stayed in until I left.

I'm reluctant. I do not want to visit where they began my indoctrination, the last place I lived before I left for good. But I think Oppa needs to see the place that, perhaps, still has a grip on him. I hold no sentiment for the place.

A few days later, Oppa says he has made arrangements for us to visit the orphanage. With the never-ending traffic, it takes us a good forty-five minutes to get there. The place is unfamiliar to me. Not the buildings, the grounds. It seems everything has been transformed into a hospital. Our guide shows us several hospital rooms with babies and toddlers in varying degrees of need. The rooms, clean, white, stark, utilitarian in their function, do not exude warmth.

It is when we walk outside, I see something familiar: a merry-go-round. I remember playing on one for hours. But it is no longer the plain rusty metal contraption I remember from my youth. It has been replaced, modernized, a jungle gym and merry-go-round in one. Shaped like a globe, six curved bars welded at the top of the center pole run vertically down to the base, and three bars run horizontally around the top half. The bottom half is open for children to enter and exit. Painted in pink, yellow and green it is more appealing than the one from my youth.

Our guide takes a picture of Oppa and I in front of the colorful ride. A reunited brother and sister smile politely with our arms around each other. Oppa's other arm holds his grey blue jacket and camera case. My hair is loose, tucked behind one ear, I have on a pink short-sleeved shirt, periwinkle blue silk skirt, a wide belt and earrings. We thank the guide for taking the picture, for her time. Oppa and I decide to take a ride on the merry-go-round.

We giggle as we maneuver our adult bodies onto the child-size contraption. Oppa gives a push. It makes us laugh, the silliness of two adults at play on a child's ride, spinning around and around. But with each rotation our laughter subsides, until there is silence. I glance over at Oppa; he looks solemnly back at me. We look away at the same moment. He jumps off the ride, steadies its momentum; I drag my sandaled feet on the ground to stop it. Oppa holds out his hand and helps me off. Holding hands, we walk away.

Part Three
OMMA

It is never too late
to be what you might have been.

GEORGE ELIOT

18

June - August 1992

Yesterday morning Omma and my sister-in-law had a terrible fight. I was climbing the stairs to Oppa's apartment, sweaty after a jog, when I heard Omma yelling and cursing. I entered the apartment in time to see eonni cover her left cheek, flee to her bedroom and slam the door behind her. Omma must have slapped her. In the throes of anger, Omma's face was ashen, her movements jerky and out of control.

"What have you done?" I shouted at her.

Omma withdrew to the corner of the living room smoked a cigarette, *opened a beer and drank it*—in the middle of the morning! She looked threateningly at eonni's bedroom door, mumbled under her breath, ignored my question.

I was shocked. Yet I'd suspected that Omma and eonni did not have much of a relationship, they rarely talked to one another. I think it's no coincidence that whenever Omma comes to stay for a time, eonnie disappears and spends a good part of the day at her friend's apartment.

I wonder if this had anything to do with the other night. Eonni and I sat together, talking. Omma decided to go to bed early. Communication with my-sister-in-law is laborious. The single word we find in the dictionary can become a sentence or a paragraph of meaning with use of pictures, symbols, hand gestures and a great deal of inference. What I understood was that she and Omma do not get along. Omma is unkind to her. She said she is not a good grandma. She has a bad temper. Eonni states Omma expects her to behave like a traditional Korean daughter-in-law. She and Oppa were very poor up until three years ago; Omma always asks Oppa for money. I listened to her complaints but I did not know what to say to her.

This is now the second time I've seen Omma unleash her anger. The first incident was during one of our evening walks several nights ago. Oppa, Omma and I were strolling through the neighborhood when we realized Omma was no longer with us. At the same moment we heard her shouting. She was still back on the street corner we had rounded which had put her out of sight. As we ran to her, I saw she was talking to an elderly man. He looked to be intoxicated. He was saying rude and hateful things to Omma about her unusable arm, but he seemed to regret his remarks. In that moment, my otherwise petite mother seemed to grow several feet as she loomed over the man, and bellowed a barrage of angry words. He held his arms up to his face, as if to shield himself from the verbal assault. It was clear to me Omma was not one to take any shit.

To have witnessed the intensity of Omma's anger toward the old man is shocking, but not for the obvious reasons.

I have noticed similarities between Omma and me. This is my personality too, of angry outbursts and out of control reactions to minor incidents.

Yesterday, on my jog through the busy streets of Seoul, I slammed my hand down on the hood of a taxi. How dare he inch ahead in the crosswalk almost hitting me! With my other hand balled into a fist, I shook it at the driver while loudly cursing him out. Even gave him the finger. Afterwards, I knew I could have handled that situation differently. He might not have seen me crossing because of the blind spot in his cab. And really, what good did it do to give him the finger? It probably meant nothing in this culture anyway.

The fight between Omma and eonni reminded me of my fights with AnnMarie. How angry I would get at her for taking my things and not returning them. Losing them even. AnnMarie found power in ignoring me, as if I didn't exist, which would send me into a rage. I'd slap, hit her, anything to get a reaction from her, to make sure she knew I was there. I didn't know how to stand up for myself with just words, so I got physical. My parents didn't listen to me when I behaved this way; the fact that I hit her put an end to all discussions, leaving me powerless and unheard. I felt my needs were not important, that my concerns were secondary within the family.

That night I went to my room to write letters to friends. I have felt the tension between Omma and eonni for some time. I knew something was afoot and that maybe the family was putting on its best face for my sake. *It is not as I stated in my earlier letters. There's trouble within the family. I think the honeymoon is over.*

⸺ꝫ⸻

I awake to find Omma and I are to take a bus to her place in Ansan for an open-ended number of days. Omma is pleasant once again. In fact, she's thrilled. She merrily packs and plans out loud all we would do together. But I'm upset. It seems to me Omma's been banished from Oppa's house, which, by extension, means I have been too.

With each creeping kilometer on the bus ride to Omma's, my irritation towards her grows. Omma holds out some *kimbop*, rice rolls with egg, spinach, spam, wrapped in seaweed, that eonni made for our trip. "Anny, you want some?" I am giving her the silent treatment. I barely shake my head.

In the distance, South Korea's wall of mountains, a hazy sentinel, surround the perimeter. Ahead, open country. Every once in a while, dazzling emerald green rice fields pop up as a visual respite for tired travelers. But these green fields are not enough of a distraction from Omma. I'm not happy with the turn this reunion has taken. I'm angry at her for causing trouble with my family. I'm dismayed knowing that my worst traits come from her.

Growing up, I yearned to find identifiable characteristics in manner and physical appearance with my adoptive family. I longed to recognize my face or body, my hair, any part of me reflected, mirrored in a parent or a sibling. I remembered how awed I was when I noticed a friend and her mother had the same smile, two sisters had similar colored and textured hair, brothers, identical stature and build. It fascinated me that Grandma and mom sigh in the same manner, an audible inhale, rather than exhale, a trait among Swedes. I ached to see the commonality between my family and me. I imagined I would be proud to discover I had the same sense of humor as dad, a creative propensity like mom, that people would comment, *you're the spittin' image of your grandma, mom.*

But I had long snuffed out those longings, dismissed them as silly. By my teens, my twenties, I was resigned to the fact my face and personality were as different from my family as east is from west.

I am ashamed of myself and that makes me angry. I'm feeling angry because I feel guilty. I am disappointed that Omma is my mother. She is not what I imagined in all the years of dreaming. She is not beautiful. Glamorous and perfectly put together she is not. Her smoking habit is offensive, not only to her health and ours, but because good mothers do not smoke.

I am embarrassed to accompany her to the market. I pretend not to know her as she makes her way through insulting and badgering the shopkeepers, proclaiming inferior produce. The vegetables are too soft, too hard, or too green, she'd say clucking her tongue, emphasizing her disapproval. All so she can haggle and pay less than what the shopkeepers request. It is too much for my Minnesota nice sensibilities. I imagine the poor shopkeepers with their turned down mouths mumbling something about a North Korean invasion on her while reluctantly accepting her measly coins.

I am surprised at the mountain of grievances building up in me as we inch towards Omma's town. Where is it coming from? And what the hell is the situation between her and eonni, anyway? Did it really warrant a slap to the face? I'm livid at being dismissed from Oppa's house, because of *her*.

I cannot help but believe that Omma is keeping something from me, holding back on the truth. I am dissatisfied with the poverty and hunger story she and Oppa told me. There has to be more to it than a year long hunger and my increasingly thin frame that turned Omma to Korean Social Service. What about Oppa? Why wasn't he put up for adoption? Did she give me away so I could have a better life? Or was it for the money she received in compensation, like my adoption papers suggested?

I am afraid to ask. I am afraid to know.

I used to believe I was tough, tried to convince myself that I could handle almost anything. But I am not. I am not strong or courageous. Instead, I am made up of Rejection and Abandonment. These twin emotions have haunted me, controlled my life since the day I was given away, and the culprit of all of this sits next to me on this tedious ride.

The bus stops at a small shopping mall in Omma's town. She jumps up, "Here Anny, we here." She grabs her bag and high-tails it to the front of the bus. First she says in Korean, and then in English, "Come, Anny, come." Those words. I have heard those words before, when I was five, six years old walking down the street with her. When I began to dawdle or took too long to catch up to her, she would yell back, *Come, Anny, come.* I had heard those words many times as a little girl up until the day I left.

Those words and this realization trigger something in me. How dare she boss me now, at twenty-nine years old? She has no right to tell me anything. In fact, she has no rights to me at all. How dare she treat me like I'm still six. Who does she think she is? Doesn't she realize the hell she put me through, giving me away like I wasn't worth anything? Fearing the day my adopted family would do the same if I didn't behave, if I didn't do as they said. Didn't she know how difficult it would be to have to be *that* good? Didn't she consider her action would take away my ability to trust, to love? Now she's been kicked out of Oppa's house. How dare she cause trouble while I'm here getting to know my family. What kind of mother gives away her six-year-old daughter? Who does that? Only a bad-tempered, uncooperative, selfish woman does that.

Omma has already scampered off the bus; she waits for me at the bottom of the bus steps. She doesn't notice my mounting anger. She's excited to bring her girl home, to feed and pamper, lie down at night beside her, just like we had done all those years ago.

Instead, I descend the bus at a run, blow past her and make a dash for the entrance to what looks like a mall. I have no idea where I'm going. I just know I don't want to go with her. Some believe we choose our parents before we are born, I don't think so, I'd never choose her. She is nothing like what I imagined her to be. I don't like her.

She shouts for me to stop, which propels me to move faster. I dash past old ladies and children who cannot guess at the oddness of this scene: a given-away daughter on the run from her just found mother.

"Anny, Anny, stop!" She's close and gaining on me. I feel a hand grab my arm. *The strength, it can't be hers.* She whirls me around, and my pent up rage finally erupts.

"Why did you give me away?" My accusing finger jabs close, close to her face, folding into a fist, itching to make contact. "What kind of a mother are you? Who gives away her fully formed daughter? Only you, you cruel, selfish bitch. Do you know the terror I went through? Do you know what you did to me? How dare you discard me like I wasn't worth anything! How dare you! Why did you give me away? Why? Why? Why?"

I cannot stop myself. I say the word over and over to draw some sort of power from it. The rhythmic beat of word and fist and finger in her face has a hypnotic effect. I am possessed. I can't stop. But my aching heart isn't satisfied.

"Fuck you. Fuck you. Fuckyoufuckyoufuckyouuuuu."

The only sound I hear is my heavy panting, though I know there is activity, noise all around us. Yet it is only Omma and I in this moment. This moment that is etched and frozen in time. It is mere seconds, but decades in the making.

Surprisingly, a gleeful smile spreads across Omma's hard-life face, transforms her. I see that she was once beautiful. "Anny," she says, laughing as she grabs her hair and pantomimes frustration and the explosive rage we both know we possess. She points to me and then she points to herself, she does this again and says, "You, me, same-same! You-me, same-same!" She laughs again and it is a laughter that seems to say, *my long lost daughter is back and she is mine. With all her flaws and imperfections and all her lost ways, I know her for she comes from me.*

"Anny, I'm sorry." She gently places her hand on my damp cheek. "I tell you everything." She takes my hand. I try to pull away but she tightens her grip. She has no intention of letting go this time. Omma looks into my teary eyes, but she sees beyond, deeper, into my center.

I dreamt of this moment. Except in my dreams, Omma is crying and begging for my forgiveness. She's prostrated at my feet, frantically clinging to my legs. I assume a look of indifference; I can't be bothered to look at her. I will let her suffer, to feel the pain of rejection. *I* walk away from her in dramatic fashion. With her arms out, she pleads for my forgiveness. In my mind's movie, the music crescendos: imagine cellos, basses, and violins straining to convey the sounds of my mother's heart breaking. I feel vindicated, control of the situation in my hands. I relish the power.

It is my moment. I can fulfill this film-fueled fantasy. I have the opportunity to reject her for giving me away.

But Omma is looking at me with shining eyes. She is looking at me with—*pride? Adoration?* Pride. Adoration. She is looking at me with *Love.*

A deafening roar thunders through my head. A jolt of electricity to my heart. My mind jumps back over the twenty-three years we did not have together. Our losses. Longings, yearnings I did not voice.

My hurting heart does not want to let go, does not want to unhand the anger and rage. It is who I am. I know no other way.

Yet, I cannot look away from her. She wears the face of love. *Love for me.*

Omma sees a shift in my eyes; she reads my thoughts. She knows *me.* My roots. I do not have to explain myself to her. She needs no dissertation of who I am. We get each other in short hand. Our blood knows the language of the other.

With tears running down my face, tears of amazement, of joy, I laugh as I grab hold of her hand, pull her towards me, incredulous. "Yes, Omma. You, me, same-same."

19

Omma's apartment complex is like many buildings throughout large cities of Korea: too many structures on too little land. These buildings are four to five stories tightly packed together, out dated, and this one looks the shabbiest. The run-down appearance disheartens me. A crumbling concrete stoop looks like a hazard waiting to happen, someone is bound to trip on the rubble, on the deteriorating steps. The length of the building on each floor has a narrow platform deck that all occupants' doors open out on. Made of concrete, the decking is cracked, the wooden railings broken or missing all together. All the apartments have small windows. Most of the doors are closed. The silence is disturbing. It seems no one lives here.

Omma's place is on the third floor on the end. We walk up three flights of rickety wooden stairs on the outside of the building. I try not to touch the railing, afraid of getting a splinter. A green plastic awning over the decking, used everywhere in Korea, casts a sickening glow on us, and the unsafe stairs. We take off our shoes on her mat outside her small north facing door, and enter a miniscule kitchen. A two-burner stove on a cement ledge, a rack of dishes, and a red plastic dishpan makes up the totality of her kitchen. Little light emanates through the tiny window, even with a bare light bulb hanging overhead. In winter, the room is unheated.

She leads me up a step and through a door to her living and sleeping area. An armoire, side table, and a washer in the corner make up her furnishings. A small window faces south.

Oppa bought the washer recently, but Omma prefers to wash her clothes by hand. On the other side of the washer is a door I thought was a closet, but inside is a toilet, her bathroom. A 1992 silk calendar of mountains with silhouetted pine trees hangs on a wall. It is similar to the one she sent me years ago.

Omma sees the look of surprise on my face; she views her surroundings through my western eyes. "It's okay," she says, stroking my arm, as if to thaw me from her cold reality. "It's a good home for me." I am speechless. Why has Oppa put her in such a small, run-down place? I'm going to have words with him when I get back to Seoul.

She likes her place. She likes living alone. Many times Oppa asked her to live with them as traditional Korean families do. But after the fight between her and eonni, I see it's probably best that they live separately.

"Anny, you sleep. I go buy some food," Omma says, getting out a pillow and blanket for me while she shops and drags home all the goods to orchestrate a feast. I cannot nap but it does feel good to rest after the temper tantrum.

Omma comes back with numerous plastic bags. Without resting, she bustles about her tiny kitchen, in her element. I sit in the doorway between the living room and kitchen and watch.

She squats down on her feet the way so many Koreans can, and quickly unpeels garlic with her good hand. In no time she has a sizable mound. When I see her pulling out the cutting board and big knife, I offer to help, but she will not let me. I think I'd just get in her way.

She washes her left foot and wraps it in a towel. And then she does something extraordinary. Her left foot is a substitute for her unusable left hand. Holding onions, cucumbers, and hot peppers steady with her foot, she cuts them into perfectly symmetrical pieces. "How can you cut everything so precisely? I can't even do that with two hands!"

Omma laughs, "No sweat, I do this way all my life." Other times, without the aid of her foot, she holds the knife steadily on an onion, cucumber, hot pepper and slices them perfectly.

She is a culinary poet in motion. Each day, Omma creates aromatic cuisines I had long forgotten or never had. My gastronomic palate takes in and rejoices at memories of never since eaten foods. The first night she refuses my protests of enough. She is on a mission. She lost twenty-three years with her hungry child and her plan is to stuff me full each day. We're eager to bridge the years of loss as quickly as we can. Being a good and dutiful Korean mother, she will do this by feeding me. I, who think about food constantly, am willing to eat all she makes.

It is a divine awakening, that first chopstick full of *bibimnangmyun;* spicy noodles, with fiery red peppers, a Korean red pepper paste, *gochujang,* cool cucumbers and a Korean pear, mixed with just enough vinegar, sugar, garlic, green onions and sesame seeds, a perfect balance between sweet and spicy. I inhale too much at once, but I care not. I moan in delirium. I have not eaten anything like it.

It is a religious conversion while eating her just-made kimchi, lightly fermented cabbage, a generous amount of red pepper flakes, *gochugaru,* garlic and ginger. I worship her *bibimbop,* a bowl of rice (bop) with vegetables of sauteed spinach and edible roots, topped with a fried egg, drizzled with kochujang, a spicy pepper sauce similar to sriracha, only ten times better.

Omma and I love all things seafood. She makes a fish soup, using a fish similar to red snapper, with jalapeno peppers, soy sauce, *gochugaru* and onions. The sweet of fish, heat of hot peppers and dense broth bring out a new level of gluttony in me.

But it is the nuclear spicy soup, *dengjangchigae,* with fermented soy beans, tofu, onions, slices of squash, clams and hot peppers, my favorite, that surprises her by how much I consume.

"You like?" I can only nod as she hurries to ladle up more. If my taste buds could sing they would have hit the high notes shattering the clay bowl my *dengjunchigae* was bubbling in.

My body goes through the shakes; I'm getting high on Korean food! I need more, a bigger fix, two servings, three serving sizes is not enough, finishing only when there is no more.

How I appreciate the Korean custom of little conversation during mealtime. I cannot handle dividing my attention with both talking and eating. Like an addict, I'm single-minded in my all-consuming need for spicy Korean cuisine over good manners, conversation.

I am not a quiet eater. While stuffing my face, I make base, primal grunts. Sheepishly, I look over at Omma. When I see her beaming face, I shrug and commence piling in the goods.

For twenty-three years I subsisted on typical American fare of bland casseroles and overly salty hot dishes alternating with good enough pizza and adequate hamburgers. They had nourished my body, but they did not fill me in this way.

My external self makes a gluttonous mess of her addictive delights. I revert to a messy six-year-old cramming my mouth with too much food, too fast. Omma sits close stroking my left leg; she needs to touch me at all times, perhaps to make sure I will not disappear on her again. She busily wipes my chin or dabs the front of my shirt as I steadily gorge on noodles or shovel spoonfuls of searing *chigae* into my insatiable mouth. I have no shame.

Omma is content to let me sleep in on mornings while she busily shops for her next round of epicurean gifts. I remain in bed long after her return, my overindulged belly fully satiated.

There is something routine and rhythmic in her actions, as if this is what she has always done every day for her daughter, without the separation of decades. Perhaps this was what her dreams were, what kept her going in those years of loss. She dreamed of feeding and lying down with her daughter, bathing her, braiding her hair so often, that when the dream became reality, she moves about as if she has done this every day.

I quickly buy into this routine, the fantasy I had sometimes allowed myself: that my real mother would pamper me and prove me worthy of her love. She would spoil me rotten and make me the center of her world.

This *is* what Omma had done all those years ago. She had indulged and taken care of me. This had been the reality of our lives over twenty-three years ago. She had engulfed me in love with food and comfort, every day, decades ago.

I remember the *sensation* of Omma's meticulous care: how she watched over me while I ate and played, dressing me in the latest trends, spoiling me with special treats of chocolates and toys. I remember the *feelings* I had had at six, of feeling safe, of feeling cherished, and of being loved.

I brought an ocean liner of longing. The love and acceptance I wanted, *needed,* is coming from the person I least expected: my mother.

Each night, Omma strokes my hair and looks over my body parts to find all the bumps and bruises she did not get to make better with hugs and kisses. She looks at my right thigh to see if the birthmark is still there.

"You remembered my birthmark!"

"Oh, sure. I never forget. You have one on your right hand too."

"Anny, you little girl time, you arm...I see picture, I so scared. I don't know white thing on your arm. I cry and cry." Omma cries again, remembering the toll it took on her. I cannot imagine her pain of seeing her child hurt and unable to do anything about it. Perhaps it was especially difficult for her, seeing my arm in a cast. She understood all too well the difficulties of a useless arm.

⁓

One morning Omma puts lotion on her face. "I have to wear lotion too or I look ten years older," I say.

Omma laughs. "Same-same, me too, I don't do, I look like old lady."

"Really? What else? How else are we alike?" I ask, sitting up on my knees to face her.

"We have same-same ears, see, down here, big." Sure enough, my lobes, that I always thought were too large, are just like Omma's.

"Our big lobes, it means good luck."

"Oh, ya? Maybe I have good luck soon," she says, and smiles.

A Vietnamese friend explained to me when I complained over my big lobes, that it signified good luck in her culture. I started rubbing my ears thereafter whenever I came up short on luck.

"How else, are we alike?".

"Young time I eat too much. One time I eat two big, big bowls of *mul naengmyung* and I no feel full!" She rounds her arm to show me the size of the bowl.

"I know what you mean! I can out eat anyone," I say with pride. I disliked going out on dates, out to dinner with boys who were full before me. Omma laughs, tickled at the thought of me out eating my dates.

"You can't be all that surprised, not with the way I've been eating the last couple of days. You've been wasting your breath, telling me to *eat some. Eat some more.*"

"You eat good, Anny. Maybe you eat too much."

We laugh. We laugh so hard, falling over on each other, delighting in our similarities.

_ɕ_

Omma suggests we go to a *jjimjilbang,* a bathhouse. She does not have anything more than a toilet; there is no room for a shower or bathtub in her apartment. For her general hygiene she washes in the kitchen space. For a thorough treatment she goes to the bathhouse. These public bathhouses are common throughout Korea. It is a do-it-yourself spa of sorts, supplied with a large locker room with showers, sauna and hot tub. A nominal fee is required for what seems like unlimited use.

I see a woman who scrubs herself thoroughly, uses the sauna, shaves, scrubs herself again, back to the sauna, relaxes on a bench, and washes herself again. She is so clean she shines, reflects light. She has been cleaning herself for hours, I think. But the minute she steps outdoors it will not take long to feel dirty again. Yet for the time being she will feel buoyant, lighter, having rid herself of the combination of sticky heat and city grime.

Omma stands naked in front of me waiting for me to undress. I get a good look at her withered pale arm. It is longer than her usable arm. Her fingers hang limp, lifeless. "Can you feel anything in your arm?" I ask, pointing to her unusable hand.

"No, no, nothing. Only one time, maybe two, three years ago I hurt. My arm hurt. That all."

"Did you ever think about having it amputated, removed?"

"No. No. I don't want that. This way I look like I have two arms."

She scrubs my back with a Korean washcloth that is more abrasive than the terrycloth washclothes I'm use to. It is the Korean version of a loofah. I like warm water and Omma prefers it hot. I scrub Omma's back. She moans with pleasure as I rub her shoulders and between her shoulder blades.

When it's my turn to be scrubbed, she strokes my long hair. "You beautiful hair, just like Omma, young time. Ipo hair, real shine, so much hair."

"Yah, it was thicker when I was young. I couldn't get my hands around it even in my early twenties, even with my big hands." Omma confirms she too had an abundance of hair. I tell her that my senior year in high school after my senior picture was taken I decided to cut my hair off.

"Why you do this?"

"I'm not sure. I think I got tired of people always complimenting my hair." By then, being noticed Korean came second to my hair. I had wondered if I used my hair as a crutch. I came to rely on the compliments and the attention my hair received which was a double-edged sword. I disliked when people commented on my locks, but if they did not, I felt invisible.

I began to wonder if I was more than my hair, or did my hair define me? On impulse, I went and got my hair cut above my shoulders. It was hideous. I wanted the feathered hairstyle that framed Farrah Fawcett's face. If by feathered I meant to have two sausage links on either side of my head from using a hot curling iron, I accomplished it. The look was awful. I became depressed. I did not get out of bed for the entire weekend. Dad came and sat by my bed and listened to my woes. How I wanted to test myself. How I needed to see if I was made of more than my hair. How I found I was not. But simply his presence, his willingness to listen to me helped me to get up for school the following Monday.

"Aigoo, long hair best. Korean woman have best hair. Beautiful long," she says with certainty.

"Maybe so, but I'm ready for a change again. I'm going to cut my hair short," I say, pantomiming scissors with my fingers cutting my hair. I bought Vanity Fair magazine not because it had a naked and pregnant picture of Demi Moore on it, but because she had a short hairstyle I liked. Omma is against it, but I will do it anyway.

"You have nice body, strong body," Omma says, studying my body.

"Yah, it's okay. But I've never liked my body."

"Why you no like?"

"I wish I were taller. Had thinner legs."

"What you like best?"

"My hands, I guess. I was a hand model for a short spell, along with some modeling and commercials."

"You model?" I like the way Omma pronounces it, *moe-dell*. "You make a lot of money?"

"When I worked it was good, but I didn't work very much." If I wanted to model seriously, an agency wanted me to lose at least ten pounds. "I couldn't do it, I like to eat." She and I laugh. But despite not loving my body, and eating too much, my body has served me well. Amazingly I am not overweight. I stopped bingeing and purging, choosing instead to run. I am physically healthy.

We continue to enjoy our showers. I close my eyes and let the near-hot water wash over my face. "You baby time, you drink my milk. I only give you my milk."

I open my eyes to see Omma cupping her breast. She looks at me earnestly. She wants me to know she took the best care of me. By feeding me mother's milk, *her milk*, she hoped to produce a strong and healthy girl. I tell her as a child I only remembered being sick once, during Christmas break, other than that I have been healthy. This makes her happy.

"My milk, good milk."

"If I ever have a baby I will do the same, give it breast milk."

"Oh sure, mother's milk best," she says. "Anny, you get married soon, have babies. You old now, find husband soon. You go back to

American and find a husband." I cannot help but laugh. We are not living in the dark ages where a woman's life depends on marriage, depends on having a husband to provide for her. Yet I know this is what is expected in her world.

"I'm not old! I am not old. Can I marry for love, or do you want me to just grab the first guy I find?"

Omma laughs. "Love best. But you marry, okay, Anny? Omma have too much trouble with men. Too much trouble. My heart hurt, too much trouble," she says shaking her head.

Around the showers are numerous benches for bathers to sit or lie down on like the elderly woman has done. She's wrapped in a white towel, with one for her hair. She looks to be asleep.

Omma sits down next to me on one of the benches. She looks at me solemnly, " I tell you something." Up until a few years ago, she was in a common law marriage for fourteen years. She said he was a good man, kind and hard working. A few summers back, a continuous pounding rain flooded a portion of the country. He was biking to work in the rain that would not let up when he was struck by a bus and died.

"Oh, Omma. I'm sorry."

"He good man. He good to me."

We sit on a bench and I dry her back and arms. "Anny, I scared to tell you about my husband."

"What? Why would you be afraid to tell me about him?" She was afraid I would disapprove of her living with a man without being legally married. She and eonni's fight was about this very issue. Eonni threatened to tell me about the relationship. Omma got upset.

"Omma, I'm in no place to judge you. Believe me. I'm happy you had someone who loved you and cared for you. You deserve to be loved, to have a good life. I wish he were still here for you," I say, taking her hand.

"He good man. He take good care of me," she says again, shaking her head remembering him, his tragic death.

After he died, his children came and took his few belongings, the little money he had. Omma received nothing.

We return from the bathhouse, after a stop at the market, and again, Omma concocts a culinary masterpiece: crabs in some sort of spicy soy sauce, which I devour greedily. Together we wash the dishes. While Omma smokes a cigarette on the landing, I rest my full belly on the warm floor with a pillow tucked under my belly. The thought, *I've got to rein in my eating*, floats past me. I dismiss it. I know I cannot. And besides, I really don't want to. I believe the steady diet of Korean food has done wonders for me. My genetic code is made up of kimchi, root vegetables, hot peppers, and garlic. Every fiber of my body and my mind is alive and energized. I feel at peace, satisfied, *whole*.

Omma comes in, takes one look at me and laughs. "Anny, you *taegi*, you eat too much." It's true I am a pig when it comes to food. I begin to reply, but Omma's face stops me. "I want tell you about my life, that okay, Anny?" She asks, solemnly. I nod my head.

Omma puts together a tray of food, ojinga and kochujang sauce, Korean melon, and my favorite drink, makuli. As if I could eat anymore. I get out our bedding like Omma suggests I do. I use the pillow for my back, and lean against the wall, ready to listen to her.

20

Countryside of Pusan, 1940

Shin-Hae Kang is small, but a mighty force. Neither her Aboji nor Omoni can keep up with her. She is a four-year-old girl living a carefree life in the countryside of Pusan, a beauty among the plain-faced children, a pearl in her Aboji's eyes. He adores his quick-think-ing, quick-moving daughter.

On a spring day she clings to her Aboji as he gathers his sack of be-longings, gives her Omma a perfunctory kiss, as he does before leaving. Once again, he must go and work at a restaurant in Pusan. In her eyes, her Aboji is a respected chef valued for his spicy of-the-earth Korean food. Thinking about his *dengjangchigae* fills her mouth with longing.

Safe travels, husband. Come back to us in due course, Shin-Hae hears her Omoni say the same farewell she has always said to her fa-ther. *Yes, of course, wife. Take good care of our tal,* daughter. Her father's dark brown eyes shine down on his daughter. Shin-Hae flashes him her radiant smile brilliant as a sunrise. It is one of the few times he grins back.

Hop on, tal. This too, they do each time. Her Aboji shifts his pack to his left side and bends down; she climbs onto his back. Her Omoni places the bundle on Shin-Hae's small back. From behind dangle two thin legs. Her Omoni walks behind them.

He carries her past the magnificent gingko tree she often plays in. He climbs the hill, around an emerald green rice paddy, to the bus stop. Shin-Hae jumps off his back and faces her father. They do not know if it will be a long wait or a short one. The bus comes when it comes, he says to her each time she inquires, as he scans the horizon. He kneels down to look at his beauty his dark brown eyes level with her eager brown ones.

He strokes her thick black braids that her mother lovingly plaits each morning. He knows by noon her braids will loosen, strands of hair will be in tangles. Her mother will again take the wooden comb to her hair, and re-braid her thick strands.

Shin-Hae can stand still no longer. She flutters her arms up and down, floats around her father, around the bus stop sign. *Nabi, nabi,* she sing-shouts. *Hey butterfly, hey butterfly, come fly over here. Yellow butterfly, white butterfly, dance while you can.*

He must fill his eyes and ears with the sights and sounds of his beautiful child. He does not know the next time he will be able to come home. He knows it will not be any time soon.

The bus is coming, come here, he says, arms out ready to catch her and hold her until the driver gives the last call to board. Shin-Hae runs and jumps on her Aboji. She squeals with delight as he moans pretending to be overpowered by her. He hugs her and whispers his love with promises of a quick return. She smiles. She knows her loving *Aboji* melts at her smile. It is the thing she alone can give him. He presses his hand to his heart. This is their unspoken language, she is precious, loved.

⁓

Shin-Hae misses her Aboji. Each morning before she rises, he is her first thought of the day. She wishes he were here to carry her on his back, to race up the hill, to throw her in the air and catch her, always he catches her. Even when he works in the rice fields or in their vegetable gardens, he makes time for her. But then she remembers her promise to her father. She must hurry and dress and be of help to her Omoni.

Once she is done with her chores, her mother sets her free to play. She runs to her gingko tree, where her father has nailed small pegs into the tree trunk for her to climb its branches. She climbs this tree often, scrabbling up as high as she can. She can almost touch the blue sky. In the evenings, she climbs to be closer to the glittering stars shining and winking at her. From high in the tree she talks to her Aboji, her messages delivered by the wind.

On a day, she stands in the crook of the gingko tree singing nabi, nabi. A yellow bird lands in a nearby branch. She is delighted to share her tree with a special visitor. She crouches down slowly and gazes at her new friend. She remains still so as not to frighten her tiny guest, but she has crouched far too long, her young limbs numb from inactivity. As she attempts to stand, she falls out of the tree and lands with a painful thud on her shoulder.

Hearing distressing cries from her daughter, her mother comes running. *Aigoo, Aigoo*, her mother begins to sob. What can she do for her poor daughter? The hospital is too far away. She has no money for this kind of problem. She tries to heal her daughter with love, holding her close until her wails fade away in fitful sleep.

Days later, aunts and uncles come for a visit. It has been many months since they last saw the little girl, how they have missed her. She favors her left arm, but this goes unnoticed by her eager relatives. They grab at her, yank and pull on her arms, vying playfully for her affection. Their laughter and play drown out the cries from the little girl. Her mother rushes to them, begs them to stop.

But it is too late. Shin Hae's arm hangs on her shoulder, useless.

᠆ᦞ

Shin-Hae sits beneath the great gingko tree. She no longer climbs its majestic limbs. She looks up into the yellow foliage wishing to send her words of longing and missing to her Aboji.

She sees a figure rise up over the hill. It is someone eager to come home. It is her father, gone too long. He sees his pearl under the great tree, and picks up speed. She is a bit taller, and her hair longer, but it is the something else he cannot comprehend. Her right arm bent, moves, propels her forward, but the left arm is stiff, stuffed into a pocket on her dress.

He takes his girl into his arms. Holding his child, his heart aches a little less. Her mother stands with head bowed, waiting to tell him of the great misfortune. She waits.

His tears have no end. He will drown. He will flood the land with his sorrow. His little girl flashes her radiant smile for him, to put his broken pieces together, but instead he weeps all the more.

Rural folks of Pusan often see the father walking about the country-side with his beauty on his back. They see him carrying her up the hill and around the rice paddy to wherever she wants to go. He carries his precious load to school each day; he is there to carry her home. He does this long after she becomes too big for him to carry. He is an Aboji torn by guilt in his inability to save his girl from misfortune. He will bear her cross. He is a wise man who knows the hardships of life and what it can do to a person; he will stave off her altered life for as long as he can.

Her broken-hearted father eases the harshness of life yet to come for his young daughter with her useless arm, but the fates are cruel; they have destined her life to be marked with never-ending struggle. Just as she makes do with her limited circumstances, using only her right hand, adapting quickly as only the young can do, misfortune strikes again.

Her mother was eager to bring to her husband and her tal, a baby brother or sister, but it is not to be. Her mother and the baby's life end in childbirth. Although this is a common occurrence among the rural people, it does not ease the grief felt by the girl and her Aboji.

She is motherless. Her Aboji is left to care for her. But how can he when much of his livelihood is spent working in the city? What is he to do with her? She needs a mother to care for her and teach her the ways only a mother can.

He decides he must marry and marry quickly. There is a woman, soon to be too old for marriage. He will marry her. She will be the mother to his little tal. She will feed and clothe and provide for her. His qualms and concerns for his tal are abated. She is in good hands.

They marry. He must leave for Pusan once again. He departs with a full heart towards his wife. She will take good care of his precious pearl.

He does not know what truly lies in his wife's heart. Her heart does not open to his tal. It remains locked with jealousy and contempt towards this girl who receives too much of her father's love.

The stepmother beats the girl, gives her little food and even less care. She makes Shin-Hae wash their laundry, help harvest the rice from the rice paddies, and cook and clean their house. The girl does all that is demanded of her.

Her stepmother will soon have a baby. The girl is excited for a brother or a sister to love. The baby, a boy, is perfect. But the stepmother will not allow the girl to touch or come near her son.

She has even more work to do. The stepmother spends her time doting and lavishing her attention on her infant son. It is a full time occupation. The girl makes her stepmother and baby brother breakfast, lunch and dinner. She has her father's gift of creating enticing and pleasing dishes. The beatings lessen when she masters her stepmother's favorites of spicy noodles, denjangchigae, and fish in spicy sauce. Her stepmother is almost kind to her as she devours bowls of the girl's labor-intensive kimchi.

The girl learns to work quickly, efficiently—her life depends on it. The beatings increase after the stepmother sees the girl's father has more love for his tal than for her and their children. The stepmother cannot bear to know he still loves his tal best even though she has given him now two children, a boy and a girl.

⎯⎯⎯ಲ⎯⎯⎯

At fifteen, Shin-Hae has grown into a beautiful young woman. Her long black hair, so thick she is unable to gather her hand around it, is kept tightly braided down to her waist. In the sunlight, her glossy hair shimmers. Her stepmother does not allow her to let her hair loose to trail down her back. Shin-Hae does not indulge in vanity. She no longer attends school. Her stepmother is often too ill to care for her children; the girl must stay home and raise her brother and sister. She has not gone to school for three years.

It is a day like any other, but for the girl, it is a day the fates prove their cruelty. Her father, the person who loves her best, dies.

They mourn his death for three days. Her *kok*, wail, is heard past the great gingko tree, over the hills and around the rice paddies and back again. The funeral banners and bier that transports his coffin is decorated with paintings of dragons and Chinese phoenixes. Many people have come to pay their respects to this honorable and humble man. A shaman is brought forth to exorcise the evil spirits from the funeral. Her stepbrother bows deeply to the coffin, throws dirt two times onto the coffin and steps away allowing others to participate in the *chwit'o* ritual.

Her sorrow has no end. Tears flow onto her Aboji's grave.

___◞___

Her stepmother has turned her out of her home. She has nowhere to go. There is an old man who might marry her. In the meantime, she can live in his house until he makes up his mind.

She has shelter but little else. She is the outlet for his angry fists, his drunken rages evident on her black and blue face and body. Sixteen-years old, she is pregnant with his child. She fears he will harm the baby. She makes the long journey back to her stepmother's home. The stepmother allows her, begrudgingly, to stay until the baby is born, but then she must leave.

One night she dreams of a big white horse. This is a good sign. She is to have a son! She will have a strong and good son. She will do everything in her power to ensure her boy grows into a good boy and a fine man. She knows this new life will bring good fortune. She thanks her *Samshin Halmoni,* her grandmother spirit, for her blessing. She folds white papers and places clean straw in the corner where she has created a shrine to her *Samshin Halmoni.* She asks for an easy birth and quick recovery.

Her auspicious dream comes true. He is a strong and healthy boy, beautiful, perfect. But she must not allow the evil spirits to find her son, or surely they will take him from her. As is the custom, she remarks upon his intellect, his stupidity. His sickly body, how weak he is! She calls him dung until the evil spirit passes over them to find and take babies elsewhere.

The stepmother obligingly creates a *kumchul* to place on the gate of their home. The straw rope is laced with red peppers to ward off evil and to reveal to others that indeed it is a boy. The kumchul will remain posted for twenty-one days. The new mother begs her step-mother to prepare rice and seaweed so she may offer it to her *Samshin Halmoni* and then she will eat it for the strength it provides.

The girl is now a mother. She has a son, which is the greatest cur-rency a poor mother can have. Even the boy's father reveres her, sees her worth; he will be good to her now. He claims he will take the best care of her and their child. But the new mother is no longer a child. She knows the heart of this man and it is no good. She will not have her son grow up believing it right to see her beaten by his father. No, she will not raise her son in a house of drink and hate.

Having a son is her best revenge against the Fates. She whispers promises in his tiny ears: she will do everything possible to give him a good life.

21

1960

They do not believe she can do the work. It is obvious she has no use of her left arm. But it is a determined young woman before them with a young son to feed. She must have this job, laundering the soldiers' uniforms.

Soon they see she is strong, capable. She can do the work of two. The other soldiers watch her toil, but teasing her is what brings them by. She makes them laugh in her eagerness to learn their off-colored words, mispronouncing their language, repeating unselfconsciously until her tongue conforms to her second language.

The soldiers keep it up, making her just mad in order to hear their handiwork crafted between Korean lips, polishing and sanding ugly language to a high sheen, her rapid-fire tongue spitting out volumes of crudeness; she has mastered the art of the soldiers' profanity. To them it is sport, a way to pass the months and years in this land inhabited by worn-out people, boundless work and backward ways they often deem inferior.

A young soldier stands back, unnoticed by this seemingly hot-tempered woman. He can see why others are entertained by her high energy, and her pretend-mad show, but he has looked into her eyes and he sees this is not the life she has chosen.

He knows she is alone, with no one but her boy. He sees a woman who must have been deeply loved, cherished; she gives the same unwavering devotion to her child. He sees all this though they have not spoken to each other. He has watched her for some time now. He knows she never stops moving. If she stops, she might not begin again. It is the need to provide for her child that creates the motion.

Shin-Hae bends over a large vat of bubbling clothes. She struggles to lift the now doubly heavy uniform out of the boiling water with her good hand. The soldier reaches for it. She looks up at him in surprise. Together they lift it out with ease and into the drying tub. They work silently until there is no more to do.

She makes ready to leave movements, says something in her language he does not understand. *Kamsahamnida,* Thank you. She is grateful for the help. Hands in his pockets, gazing down at the ground, he contemplates his next move. He looks in her direction and gives her a shy smile. He watches as she walks the worn path to her village.

The next week he is waiting for her. Again he helps her. No one disturbs the two, for the soldiers see something special developing between these two unlikely people: a Korean woman with an unusable left arm and a shy, quiet soldier who looks…Korean? American Indian?

Shin-Hae's work is finished. She pantomimes eating gestures. Would he like something to eat? He would. She leads him along the path to her small house. Here, she creates for him a heaping bowl of bibimnaengmian, spicy noodles fit to feed kings and shamans. He cannot stop taking in the siren heat, sweet and sour of the noodles, nor does he try. She brings him more. More.

_6

At first, he is protective in sharing his history, his life; she is patient. He loves her for seeking out the better within him. His kindness and quiet ways wins her heart. She does not hold back; she knows him to be true. He will do his best for her.

He speaks freely of his hobbies. His favorite pastime, reading, especially of ancient places and far away destinations he hopes to some day visit. He speaks of the two traveling together. He mentions the reservation life of his grandparents in Pennsylvania. He would like to bring her to America.

He teaches her the English words of his country. Soon they converse in two languages, mixed in with a coded third language spoken between two people in love.

In her small home, the love between a half Caucasian, half Indian man and a Korean woman blooms and grows. He came to this land innocent to the secret ways of love and belonging. At twenty-five he feels the bonds a husband feels for a wife. He feels at home. His Indian features are not unlike the faces of the people of this country. His gentle ways and abiding respect for the people have won him a place among them. It is more than he has received in his own country.

In a short time they have built a good life. Together they find a common desire in giving to others less fortunate. The people of Korea continue to feel the effects of the Korean War. There are leagues of poor and hungry. Beggars come often to their village. The young lovers cook pots of Korean rice, and once it has cooled, they pour the nourishment into the hands of those that have gone without for much too long. The young lovers feel blessed and grateful to give what they have.

On a day, bad news arrives from headquarters in America. The news crosses turbulent waters, skims over mountains, whirls around rice paddies, touches down at the base. Here the unfortunate news is met with suspended disbelief. All that he has, all he has found will soon disappear. He is to be transferred back to the states. On heavy feet he walks the worn path to their house.

He wants to marry her, leave for America together. But there is no place for her son. She will not leave her son. He will return to his country, to Pennsylvania, without her, though she is carrying his child. If she is a girl, he asks she be named Anny.

Long after the train has carried him away, she stands on the tracks hand on her round belly, silently calling him back.

꒦

Her son is away at school, her daughter, Anny, five, plays nearby.

Shin-Hae does not see them coming, an American husband and wife from the army base. They come with big smiles.

Anny is nearby running between the rows of drying clothes hung on the line, either chasing or being chased by her friends. She hears her daughter's laughter, which always brightens her spirits despite the many more loads of clothes before her. She and a few women from the area launder the Americans' uniforms.

The women busily gossip as they plunge their reddened arms into the bubbling brew, pull out the clothes and squeeze them through a wringer that leaves them just-damp for hanging. Shin-Hae prefers to wash alone today. The only conversation she took part in was when Anny came to help. Her daughter had informed her she was going to be a laundry lady when she grew up. How Shin-Hae laughed. To prove this, Anny tried to lift one of the weighted uniforms to hang, grimacing and groaning, making her laugh all the more. She playfully shooed her daughter away.

The American man and woman call out a greeting to the other women, but do not stop until they stand in front of her. The women stop their conversations mid sentence. They sense a shift in the air, something unpleasant.

In stilted Korean the man speaks first. *Anyounghaseyo, Ajima, peace be with you.* Shin-Hae stops working and greets the man without looking at him. The woman speaks slowly in Korean. *You have a beautiful little girl. How old is she, five, six years old? I noticed her playing in the fields near the army base and I see her often here with you on laundry day. I see the resemblance between the two of you.* Shin-Hae smiles. *We noticed she doesn't go to school.* Her smile disappears. *We know a way she can go to school, where she can get a fine education.* The woman has her attention. *It is in a place called America.* She knew all about America from stories her American sergeant friend had told her. But what did she mean Anny can go to school there?

There are many American families who want children, but cannot have them. I am sure your daughter could be adopted into such a family. What is this adoption? The woman explains: *Bring your daughter to the city, to Korean Social Service.* She gives her the address on a small white card. *Tell them you want to 'put your child up for adoption' and they will do the rest.*

Does this mean give her away? To another family? Never see her again? The man and the woman nod their heads in acknowledgement. *It is the best thing you would be doing for your child. She would—*

Shin-Hae picks up the thick wooden paddle used to stir and beat out the dirt and grime in the uniforms. She holds it high over her head. She swings the stick just missing the woman. The man grabs his wife in time, getting out of the angry woman's path. She screams in English every curse word she has learned, switches to Korean curses, back to English. She continues to hack the air with the paddle as the man and woman dodge her weapon. The other mothers scramble to help her. Without hearing the foreigners' words, they understand the two have not come in peace. They join in, shouting and attempting to splash dirty wash water on the intruders. Shin-Hae chases after them with her stick, continues screaming obscenities, until the man and the woman disappear into the safety of their army.

The battle is over. The children have long ceased their playing. They stand wide-eyed, looking at the outburst of violence, wash water turned to muddy pools, clothes launched at the intended targets lie in heaps, in the dirt. Clean clothes once hung entangled on the ground.

The women speak at once. *What did they want with Anny? Were they going to take her? I hear they do that, they befriend us and then they steal our children and....*

Shin Hae walks wearily towards her daughter. She wants to take her home, to forget this bizarre occurrence. *Come, Anny, come. Let us go home.*

But once a seed is planted, there is a chance it will grow.

Shin Hae tries not to dwell on that strange day. She is preoccupied in feeding, clothing, sending her bright son to school, and caring for her unschooled daughter. It preys on her, the guilt, thoughts of Anny unable to attend school. Even to have her son away at school is becoming difficult. Between the laundry at the army base and working the rice fields with her one good arm, she barely gets by.

It was not always this way. There was a time, not long ago, when her life was simple and filled with ease and comfort. A housekeeper to do the work that consumes her now, her days free for shopping at the market, weekly visits to the hair salon for Anny and herself, spoiling her daughter with treats of sweets and pretty things.

She was well provided for by her California friend, a sergeant, whom she met when Anny was two. Shin-Hae knew she was not the love of his life. He was married to a nurse back in California. He talked of her often and she came to know second hand his ambitious wife who could not have children. She knew he sent his wife pictures of Anny.

Anny at two, dancing on the floor at the mess hall the night they met; Anny, four, freshly turned out from the beauty salon with her beehive hair do, and, most recently, Anny wearing a beautiful pink hanbok dress he bought her. She knew he was taken with her daughter from the moment he saw chubby Anny on the dance floor four years ago. She was filled with pride watching her fearless daughter dance and showing off for all the soldiers who were out for fun that sweet summer night. He danced with Anny, making her giggle and run about gleefully. He insisted on walking them home afterwards with a full moon lighting their way. He carried her sleeping daughter into her home, gently settled her on the floor in the corner. He returned the next day with gifts for Anny: candy and popcorn and a doll with blondehair and blueeyes. He brought Shin-Hae flowers.

He hinted how much his wife would love Anny. She would lack nothing. They could give her everything and more. To Shin-Hae this was just talk. It was two people keeping each other company, brought together by circumstances that would soon change. He would be re-located eventually, as all soldiers were at some point or another. She indulged his fantasy of the life Anny could live in California.

But now, six months later he was gone to another country; her circumstances greatly altered. No more housekeeper, no more sweets, no more treats, no more indulgences. Anny seemed unfazed, forgetting him after asking so many times where was he, and hearing only I don't know.

Shin Hae did not see that what the American couple suggested, and the wishes of the California friend who treated Anny like his own, were not dissimilar. But the couple had threatened her in ways that wishful fantasy had not. They haunted her in sleep and throughout her days. Other Americans expressed similar unsolicited opinions, their words, tone filled with judgment and recrimination. They stopped her on the path between the Army base and the village. They found her at the market and insinuated she was selfish for wanting to keep her child. They kept up their campaign, steadily whittling away her confidence. *She should be in school. Being a good mother means sending your daughter to school. A good mother would put her child's needs over her own desires. She was not a good mother. No good. No good.*

And she believed them. Who was she to keep a girl who easily gained attention from both foreigners and her people? She was proud to take Anny to the market, to the beauty salon, to Pusan, to visit the remainder of her small clan, to any place. She swelled with pride to have a daughter rewarded with such good fortune.

They assured her she would be adopted immediately. They told her she was making an unselfish decision…. *How lucky your daughter is to have a thoughtful mother like you…Good mother…Good mother….*

⤐

The good mother lies alone in the corner where her only daughter once slept. The California friend comes back from another country. His excited footsteps can be heard inside the darkened house. He knocks, and knocks again. She does not come to the door. He is ready to leave, but the faintest sound stops him. Is it crying he hears? He slides the door open and stands in dismay at the transformation. He looks at the face of a mother who no longer believes in sunshine, light, or laughter.

As she tells him what she has done, he cries out in disbelief.

22

I look at Omma for what seems a long time. "So...so, these people came up to you and made this judgment about you...that if you were really a good mother, you'd put me up for adoption?"

"Omma so mad I kick them out. Omma run after they screaming, they say this to me. They crazy. I tell them, get out! Go away!" But they did not let up.

Omma cries while retelling her ordeal. "I...I...I'm so sorry, Omma. I had no idea." I stroke her leg as she dabs at her face. I cannot be bothered with wiping my tears away, the tears, a mixture of sorrow and indignation. How dared they say such things to Omma. I cannot imagine this happening if the situation were reversed, a Korean serviceman and woman telling an American mother to give up her child. It would never happen.

"I want to go for a walk."

"But it's night time, Anny, dark outside now."

"I don't care. I need to go out for a bit." Omma agrees to the walk. She will not let me go by myself. With few streetlights our walk is nearly in darkness, which I am grateful for. I can let the tears flow without feeling self-conscious of others we might pass on the street. But no one is out. They are tucked in bed having sweet dreams.

Omma takes my hand as we make our way the streets. I cannot find words for how I feel. I am afraid I will unleash my sorrow-rage. I would if I were face to face with the people who told my mother to give me up for adoption.

By the time we get back to her place, the city is fast asleep, but I am still mulling things over. We sit in silence. I drink some makuli and try to eat ojinga. I'm not hungry, yet it gives me something to do. The food does not go down easily.

My father. I am stunned to hear the story of my father. Omma and my father loved each other. It was mutual. For a time, after he returned to Pennsylvania, they wrote letters to one other. She told him all about me. I was named Anny just like he wished.

"How long did you write to each other?" I ask, picturing Omma sitting under a tree reading his letters.

"Long time. I have many many letters," she says, measuring an inch with her fingers to show me the sizeable stack she received from him.

"Oh, can I see them? Can I read them?"

"No, no have," she says. "My heart hurt so much. He want me come to America but not Oppa. One day I get mad. I burn his letters." She moved away and never again had contact with my father.

I understand how Omma must have felt; a feeling of abandonment. Maybe even *screw you. I don't need you or the train you left on.* I am the same way. If I didn't like the apartment I lived in, I picked up and moved. Didn't care for the job, I found a new one. If the relationship wasn't working, there was always another fish swimming by. She left the village at some point and went to Seoul to get a fresh start.

"Oh, he a good man. Good, good man," Omma says, knowing no other words, superlatives, to describe him. "Never met a better man," she claims, not even her husband who died biking to work in the rain.

At first, I have a hard time believing this. It seemed the literature and research stated that soldiers took advantage of the situation here. Didn't they ransack the country and litter the land with Amerasian babies?—*dust of the streets*, as Koreans referred to the mixed race children. Because of this belief, I had difficulty with anyone in uniform. I saw them as abusers of power, hell bent on deflowering and then discarding women at their pleasure. I had come to think of my father as this type of man, of most men fitting in this category, walking libidos with nothing on their brain but the next conquest. As I got older, I saw men as the enemy; I would not fall for their ruse. I could play their game better. I became an expert at having them and leaving them. I was on to the next without a backward glance. This was my retaliation, my way of getting back at men, especially my father. It was an absurd way to live.

But to hear my father was a good man, to hear he loved my mother, this has the healing properties that no amount of therapy could cure. If my father could love, then that half of him dwelling in me might possibly do the same. If he loved my mother and I was conceived out of love, rather than out of lust and take, than I might have the ability to love too. This is what a given-away girl with a nearly impenetrable fortress of a heart needed to know.

My father's heritage intrigues me. His grandparents were Native American. Omma did not know whether it was on his father or mother's side of the family. That makes me a quarter Indian. I have thought there was something *other*, something *more* than Korean features that made up my face. I noticed my Indian features more when I was younger, usually on waking, when I still looked sleepy, or when I was tired. Something about the broad cheekbones and the angle of my nose. I'm proud to know I have Indian blood in me. Several times I considered teaching on a reservation in Minnesota or out in the Dakotas. I liked to think it was the latent Native American in me feeling the pull of reservation life, but in truth, I have always been drawn to those who are marginalized.

Later, when I return to Minnesota, I will try to pinpoint who the native people of Pennsylvania are. I am told possibly Seneca or Oneida, but in 1830 the American government relocated thousands of native people to Oklahoma. This has come to be known as the Trail of Tears. Because of this shameful occurrence, there is no dominant tribe in Pennsylvania.

Omma cannot recall my father's name. Korean's customarily refer to his, her spouse by title, *husband, wife* rather than the Western custom of first names. She only remembers his surname started with "Mc" or "Mac," as in McBride or MacDonald. I fancy myself part Irish or Scottish.

So, my identity continues to take shape: I am half Korean, a quarter Indian and a quarter Caucasian. I don't know if I will ever find my father or know anything more about him. But I hope for the day our lives converge and I can proudly tell him I am his daughter, and that I, too, love to read and long to travel the world.

⁓

I caress Omma's ancient-young face, still baby soft at fifty-six. I gaze into the face of a fierce warrior mother who committed a feat so great, even the gods have bowed their heads in respect. It is the face of a woman, who against her will knows too intimately the hardship, the ugliness of life, of crushing loss, mistreatment, and unrelenting work. We are made up of our experiences, but I cannot help believe Omma could still be herself without all the hard times thrown on her. We cry and hold each other in the hopes we can squeeze out some of our deepest sorrows.

Never have I been so comfortable around another person as I am with Omma. It is the first time in my life I am completely and thoroughly relaxed in the presence of another. Accepted unequivocally.

No apologies needed. It is amazing that two decades of time, different languages and vastly different life experiences cannot keep us at arms length.

I am not a guest in her home. I am not a visitor staying a short while, enough to share pleasantries, tidbits of trivial interests to regale others with once I return home. There are no barriers, no secrets, or artifice between us. We are made up of the same nerves and fibers. She is my mother. I am her daughter.

Did she do right putting me up for adoption? Many times during our days together and into our future, she will examine, replay, and question her decision, which changed our lives. But with circumstances as they were, she was a mother who made the ultimate sacrifice. It is she who remains haunted, breaking down in despair at a choice that I now know she did not make lightly, did not make for her own gain. I assure her I understand. It was an act of selfless love. It was an act of love so deep no mortal ought to attempt. She had nothing else to give me, except the one thing she still had the power to give: A new life.

It is I who want to make life better for her. But what can I do? Omma assures me that Oppa takes good care of her. I want to do something to honor her for her sacrifice. And I want her to know her life has value, that her presence here has been noticed. I want to erase the sorrowful memories that make up her life. I want to give her new memories, happy ones, along with a life of comfort, ease, joy, oh, boundless joy.

I will do something, some day, to pay homage to her. I will do something, Omma. I promise you, I will do something.

Omma's life has been a struggle, a hardship. She is a warrior, a fighter, a survivor. I think in many ways I could not endure what she has. Yet,

I am my mother's daughter. I am beginning to believe I have an inner warrior in me too. I have never been tested in the ways my mother has and I cannot imagine that I will. But I believe I can overcome, survive anything. We are same-same.

Later that evening, long after our pillow talk in our own brand of language, as I gaze at my mother's face, I notice the lines of hard life have softened, that she sleeps in peace. I think about her as a four-year-old girl and how her life changed the moment she dislocated her shoulder. It is epic in scope to think that her life could have been drastically different. The choices of her narrow life might have been broader on which a once beautiful, bright and vivacious girl could have set her sights. She would have had more, and better marriage prospects from worthy men, if her father had not died in her prime. But, of course, that means our lives would have followed a different course. Oppa and I would be different versions of ourselves. I do not suppose Omma would have met my father, which then means I would not be here, or I would be a different version of myself. And, I would not have been adopted.

Because of this tragic circumstance, Omma losing the use of her arm, that singular event determined what her life would be, as well as Oppa's and mine. What my life has been, and is, is a life of plenty. I have had twenty-nine good years. I have no regrets for myself. But my breath catches when I think that my good life was on the back of Omma's life of misfortune.

On another night, Omma and I, again, are lying on the floor sharing more of our life stories. It comes to me. I sit up and I pull her to a sitting position. I try to conjure up my best Korean self. I kneel down in front of her and extend a deep bow. As my forehead touches the floor, I say what is in my heart. *Kamsahashimnika, Omma.* Thank you. *Kamsahashimnika.* I come up to a kneeling position and take in her face. She is crying. I take her hand into both of mine and begin to cry. With tears streaming down our cheeks, we hold each other and whisper over and over, *Saraenghamnida. Saraenghamnida. Saraenghamnida.* I love you. I love you. I love you.

23

Once I return to Oppa's house, where Omma stays the night and returns to her place, I tell him I know Omma's story. I cry all over again. He does too. The crying that will never end.

I am sad for Omma that she's alone. I say to him that I hope he and eonni, my nieces, will go see her periodically. It is important to try to repair the rift between Omma and eonni. I cannot imagine living with this type of friction among family members. Oppa knows of my relationship with my American mom and AnnMarie and how we are trying to come together after years of discord. He hears me. He understands.

We drive to Ansan, my nieces, eonni, Oppa and I. Omma does not know we are coming which I am not sure is a good idea. Shouldn't we call first to make sure she will be there? We are blocks from her place when Ah Young spots her walking back from the market. I'm surprised she was able to pick her out among so many people. Omma is surprised into silence at the sight of all of us. She insists on walking back to her place rather than riding with us. We will meet her there. Ah Hee will walk with her.

Once settled in Omma's house, she and eonni make small talk. Eonni bows to Omma. I think it is a good sign. The three of them talk. My nieces and I sit and silently eat watermelon.

⁓

Omma and I are back at Karak Market. We make our way through the narrow aisles. I am no longer embarrassed to be here with her. She knows what she is doing. She taps on a watermelon and listens, "This one ripe," she says confidently. She knows the price of things and she will not pay more than she needs.

I navigate through the market like a native, bumping and getting into other people's space. I am unfazed when people shove me out of the way.

While waiting to place our fish order, Korean's version of sushi, I notice a little boy at the next table. More accurately, I notice something *on* the little boy, *a live thing on* his arm. My eyes have not failed me. It is a *very alive baby octopus*. Stuck on the boy's chubby arm. And it will not come unstuck from the boy's chubby arm. He tries to pull it off, but the tentacles adhere like glue.

Omma sees my gaped expression, looks over at the boy. She laughs. "You baby time, you like so much. You play with baby octopus, same-same," she says pointing to the boy. "Octopus move up you arm and stick to you, too."

"WHAT? I literally played with it, like it was a pet?" I might have shouted.

"Oh, sure, you like so much," she says. I have a hard time believing this, but no memories come to me to refute this. Yet I cannot look away from the boy who is clearly enjoying his pet.

"Good to eat, too," Omma says, giving me a mischievous grin.

She orders raw fish this and raw fish that. The ajimma efficiently doles out a generous bowl of kochujang paste along with some lettuce leaves. The scent of kochujang sauce wafts towards me making my mouth water. In no time she sets down a plate under my nose. On the plate there is *movement*, by which I mean, the food we're suppose to eat is *moving*. I'm not keen on food that moves. It means my food is alive. Sure enough, a baby octopus whose tentacles have been cut into *bite size pieces* is *moving*. I look over at the boy and think, so help me if it's the one he had on his arm...but no, he's still pulling at the octopus, it's tentacles stretched to twice its length.

The octopus on the boy, the active live meal in front of me does not sit well with me, but strangely, I am fascinated. Omma holds one between her chopsticks. It is squirming. I think it is upset. I cannot believe I'm contemplating the emotional well being of what is supposed to be food.

"It's still alive," I say, none too happily.

"No, no alive," Omma assures me. "Eat some," she says, moving the plate closer to me. It has been a while since she needed to encourage me to eat. Or that I didn't greedily start in on the food. Too many times at her place I showed my rude manners by beginning without the customary politeness of waiting for her to take the first taste.

But eat, I cannot. Omma won't take another bite unless I have some. I have to do this. It'll hurt her feelings if I do not.

I have never chewed food as quickly as I did with the octopus. I did not want to feel the thing moving in my mouth. I chewed it thoroughly, too, not wanting to feel it in my stomach. It is my one obligatory bite. My stomach roils a bit. Until I see the next dish, a plate of bright orange. It is the mung gi I love. Omma pushes the plate towards me.

"Eat," she says.

"Okay, Omma, if you say so."

—◌—

On a lazy night, Omma and I return from our nightly walk when something on television catches my eye. We missed most of what appears to be a documentary. I cannot understand a word of it; Omma explains the images, translates what the narrator said.

They are called *haenyeo,* or sea women. They live on Cheju Island, a short flight south from Seoul, where Koreans escape for vacation. The island, much like the Hawaiian Islands, is made up of volcanic lava, and is also similar in terrain and climate.

Haenyeos make their living searching and harvesting seafood from the bottom of the ocean in the Korea Strait. By *free diving.* Just like the haenyeos before them, they use *no* breathing apparatus, only a facemask and wet suit. They can dive more than thirty feet and hold their breath for over two minutes! They use sharp tools to scrape abalone and conch and other delicacies from the water. They sell most of what they make, some of it eaten on the spot by tourists who come to watch the women haul in their bounty in metal nets. They clean and cut up the catch on nearby rocks to awed tourists.

I imagine all those years ago, and maybe currently, the women did not have the luxury of owning or purchasing boats or fishing equipment. But being resourceful women, they made the best of what they had. Themselves.

Most of the haenyeos range in age from forty to mid-sixties, the oldest is in her eighties! "Aigoo," Omma says, once she hears this on the program.

"Oh, my god, that's remarkable." I say, amazed. "I want to do that!"

"You swim good, Anny?" I tell her I can swim, that I was on the swim team in junior high and that I've always been a strong swimmer. It is probably the thing I can do best. I tell her about scuba diving and snorkeling and that I have always been game to do anything connected with water.

"Then you can be haenyeo, no problem this," she says, in her matter of fact can-do attitude.

I'm enamored, fascinated by these women. I know if I had remained in Korea I would have wanted to be a sea woman. With my love for all things water, it would have been the ideal work for me. I imagine it a dangerous and difficult occupation which is why I respect what they do all the more. I admire their strength and also their collegial spirit; they sit together after a hard day's work laughing and good-naturally joking with one another. A sisterhood forged by the offerings of the sea.

I will have a chance to see these remarkable women with my daughter long in the future. A memory I will treasure.

⁖

August, 1992

On one of the last days, before I return to Minnesota, the three of us visit a traditional Korean Folk Village. Omma and Oppa have mentioned this village a number of times. They are proud of this place that represents a way of life that's all but disappearing.

Ever since I was young I have been interested in the history of various civilizations, particularly how people lived and what they did to survive. I remember my mom reading to the four of us from the *Little House in the Big Woods* series. Each night we'd climb onto one of our beds, peered over mom's shoulder to get a look at the illustrations, and followed along as she read out loud Laura Ingalls Wilder's life as a pioneer girl growing up in the Midwest. Once I learned to read I plowed through her books a number of times. We even visited one of hers and Almanzo's homes. I was beside myself at the thought of walking the same ground that Laura walked. That one time Laura had touched this and that.

The idea that rugged pioneers were willing to stake their lives on a new place in the hopes of creating a home, a new life, through hard work, I appreciated.

I also delighted in Laura's adventures and spunky attitude. Maybe I was a bit obsessed with her, dressing up as Laura for Halloween, hair in braids, dressed in a calico skirt and matching bonnet mom made for me. I hold dear all the countless hours DebbieDeannePeggy and I played Pioneers, with Tim as Pa, I was usually Ma. Our picnic table served as the covered wagon, the annex behind the garage, our log cabin. I could not get enough of reliving that life.

Here is my opportunity to see what life was like for my ancestors, how they lived long ago, and perhaps how some traditions have prevailed and are carried forth today. Inside the entrance of the village, carved masks sit on top of tall wooden totem poles, with Chinese characters etched down the length of each pole. Omma tells me the masks are to ward off evil, bad luck. But the prominent feature is a large boulder where small rocks and stones are randomly stacked like a cairn. More stones are piled on the ground. It's cordoned off by thick rope. Omma tells me that people find a stone and place it in this shrine-like area in the hope of making their dream come true or as a prayer to ancestors.

Omma searches for a small stone so I can make a prayerful wish. She finds one and gives it to me. "You say good luck for you," Omma says. "Maybe thank you, to mother, father," she suggests.

Under different circumstances I might have wished for money, a thinner body, Mr. Right, but instead I say a silent prayer, *Please look after Omma and Oppa. Thank you.* I place the stone on the very top of the mound, holding my breath until I'm confident the stone will stay. Oppa wants to take a photograph after I already placed the stone. I re-enact the event by pretending to place the already laid stone on top of the pile.

I'm taken with the thatched roofed homes, *choga-jib,* where the farmers lived, as well as the courtyards, raised wooden walkways which seems sensible as a way to avoid tracking mud, snow into homes.

Ubiquitous throughout Korea and abundant in the village are enormous brown clay pots, where kimchi and fermented soybean paste are stored. I try out a tall stand-up mortar and pestle they used to grind rice in. I ham it up for Omma who laughs at my over performance, grimacing and groaning as I lift the heavy pestle. Oppa captures my clowning moment in a photograph. I do respect the back breaking work that was required, that many still do. Strange to believe, but I cannot help think I would have liked living this way.

Oppa wants us to see the folk drummers perform *Pungmul,* Korean folk music. He tells me the drummers danced and drummed during the harvest season and other agricultural occasions. We sit with other spectators in an open arena, four levels of stone seating around the perimeter. A good crowd has gathered.

I hear the drums before I see them. A dozen drummers appear from one end of the arena. They wear colorful clothing in red, blue and yellow with white pants. On their heads are giant pompoms of red, yellow, white, which I think might represent a flower, maybe chrysanthemums. Other dancers wear black hats with long white streamers. The dancers whirl their heads at a dizzying speed making the streamers dance and twirl, never tangling them, which in itself is impressive. It is a stunning show.

We wander through an area where Korean pottery is made. The light green jade celadon color, *cheong-ja,* is distinctive and beautiful to behold. This technique of glazing began in the mid-tenth century when ceramics were used in ritual ceremonies. This celadon color I will forever associate with Korea.

"Anny, you try it on," I hear Omma say. I have gone ahead of her so I'm not sure what she means. She's looking off to her right, she's spotted a stand where you can try on traditional Korean hanboks. This unsuspecting girl who came to learn something about the Korean culture is now looking at her excited Omma who is holding up a traditional Korean *wedding* hanbok.

"Oh, that's okay, I don't think so." I say, looking to Oppa to rescue me. Who does nothing but smile.

"Anny, you try on," she says, as if she didn't hear me decline her order.

The Korean wedding dress is red, with extra long wide striped sleeves that drape when hands come together. The stripes are colorful bands, light green, white, blue, red and yellow. Embroidered on the ends of the over-sized sleeves, red flowers. I half-heartedly don the apparel. "Put this on, too." Omma wants me to wear a matching headpiece decorated with faux stones that resembles a large pincushion. This piece sits near the front of the bride's head with her long hair coiled in a bun at the nape of her neck. A colorful tassel dangles over my forehead.

This headpiece is not made for an unconventional half Korean girl who recently cut her hair short in the likes of the latest Demi Moore style. Omma tries to slick my hair under the headpiece, but my uncooperative short bangs refuse to conform, a portion of hair slips out, spills over my forehead. I am a far cry from a traditional Korean girl.

Omma does not mind. Her eyes sparkle. She takes me in, absorbs and holds this image of me in the wedding dress. I cross my arms in a way I imagine a Korean bride might. She is easily amused by my act. "Ipo, Anny, ipo. You marry time, you wear this." I half-heartedly smile. *I doubt it,* I think to myself. However, in three years Omma and my nieces will attend my wedding where I wear a *red* dress, a nod to the Korean custom.

I take a last photograph of Omma and Oppa before my return to Minnesota. They stand in a grove of young trees. The dappled foliage dots the ground around them in light and dark. Oppa puts his arm snugly around our mother. Omma's pink blouse enhances her sun kissed skin, her eyes shine bright behind gold-rimmed glasses.

Oppa wears a straw hat with a blue and white cotton band on the crown, a camera around his neck. Behind them in the background, is a traditional structure, the exit, painted in gold and maroon.

I look through the tiny opening in the camera. "Kimchi," I say, like we do each time our picture is taken.

Long in the future I will delight in sharing with my husband, my two children, all the photographs and stories of my time with my long-separated family. "She is your *Halmoni,* grandma. He is your *Samchon,* uncle," I will say with pride. Gratitude. "Let me tell you about our family."

Oppa smiles, and says kimchi. Amidst the trees that shade them, Omma's smile illuminates the shadows. She has her son by her side. Her daughter is in front of her taking a picture for posterity. Her children. Her family.

For this moment, this last moment, I convince myself it was always this way.

Acknowledgments

They say it takes a community to write a book. A tribe helped me in this writing endeavor.

I wrote this book for you, Omma. I wish life had been better to you. You deserved so much more.

This book is for you, Oppa. Thank you for never forgetting. For taking good care of our mother.

To my husband, Jon Gjerde, this book could not have been written without your encouragement, support and belief in me. Not only did you build me a beautiful house but you also built me a writing room! Some would call that pressure. I know I did. Thank you. You are my home.

Thank you to my parents, Lynn and Janice Strand, for instilling the important values. Mom, I miss your cooking and your creativity in decorating. To my in-laws, Clint and Ione Gjerde, thank you for your love and support, not to mention the fine work in creating your progeny, Jon.

To Heidi Fokken, your steadfast care during the young years, befriending Omma when she visited, your kindness to my kids, and for being my dear friend, thank you. You continue to make all the difference.

Mary and Dick Strand, thank you for the use of the bunkhouse on the island so I could attend a writing workshop. Thank you for all your support.

To my kind and loving children, Lila and Oliver Swenson, thanks for listening countless times to my stories. Mostly though, I appreciate you choosing me as your mother.

Tami Mohamed Brown! Your guidance and skill in editing this beast has made this book better than I could have dreamed. Also, a huge thank-you for writing the back cover summary and capturing the essence of my story. I hope my story did it justice!

Don't we love the cover? Thanks to Jenn Nienaber's design talent, it is better than I could have imagined. Thank you.

To Jeanne Gallagher, whose discerning eye caught numerous errors in the final edit, thank you for your time, and for believing in my story from the beginning.

Thank you, Mary Anne Radmacher for the use of your beautiful words. Days after returning from Korea, I found your words on a card and they continue to echo what is in my heart.

To my writing group: Tami M. Brown, Jeanne Gallagher, Patsy Kahmann, Liz Sjaarstad, Jenn Nienaber, Rachel Guvenc, Laura Fanucci, and Kris Woll, I have appreciated your spot-on critiques, suggestions, and encouragement to keep writing.

Thanks to early readers, Molly Gage, Jill Rost, Jo Lindstrom, Denese Sanders, and Sandy Swenson, your enthusiasm and interest in my story was needed to keep me going. Becky Falk and Lisa Knighten, thanks for coming to my first reading. To Laura Flynn thanks for your guidance with the manuscript early on. A big thank you to my book club, mah-jong players, Listen to Your Mother story-tellers, friends, family and teaching colleagues, for coming to my readings, for interest in my book. Thank you, David Mura, for nurturing and bringing into the light a community for writers of color.

My running music before sitting down to write, Dixie Chicks, John Meyer, U2, The Eagles, Cowboy Junkies, and Adele, always helped.

French roast coffee. Chocolate. Thank you for existing.

And to my faithful dog, Otto, you're the best running boy, and good listener of first drafts. Now come and get a treat.